GOD,
THE DEVIL,
and
HARRY POTTER

Also by

JOHN KILLINGER

Ten Things I Learned Wrong from a Conservative Church
Enter Every Trembling Heart
Lost in Wonder, Love, and Praise

GOD, THE DEVIL, and HARRY POTTER

A CHRISTIAN MINISTER'S DEFENSE OF THE BELOVED NOVELS

∞

JOHN KILLINGER

THOMAS DUNNE BOOKS
ST. MARTIN'S GRIFFIN ♏ NEW YORK

THOMAS DUNNE BOOKS.
An imprint of St. Martin's Press.

www.stmartins.com

Title page photography courtesy of freestockphotos.com

Book design by Jonathan Bennett

Library of Congress Cataloging-in-Publication Data

Killinger, John.
    God, the devil, and Harry Potter : a Christian minister's defense of the beloved novels / John Killinger.—1st ed.
        p. cm.
    ISBN 0-312-30869-8 (hc)
    ISBN 0-312-30871-X (pbk)
    1. Rowling, J. K.—Religion. 2. Christian fiction, English—History and criticism. 3. Children's stories, English—History and criticism. 4. Fantasy fiction, English—History and criticism. 5. Rowling, J. K.—Characters—Harry Potter. 6. Potter, Harry (Fictitious character) 7. Christianity and literature. 8. Devil in literature. 9. God in literature. I. Title.

PR6068.O93 Z737 2003
823'.914—dc21   2002034746

First St. Martin's Griffin Edition: April 2004

10 9 8 7 6 5 4 3 2 1

For
Arthur and Charles Salutksy
and James D. Smith,
my good friends when I was
Harry Potter's age,
and
Thelma Hayes Herrin,
who was our devoted teacher
and has faithfully kept up
with all of us ever since

CONTENTS

GOD,
The DEVIL,
and
HARRY POTTER

INTRODUCTION

The appearance of Harry Potter has been one of the most exciting events in publishing history. The first Potter novel, *Harry Potter and the Sorcerer's Stone,* was turned down by several publishers for being either too literary or too long or both. But when it appeared in bookstores it became an overnight sensation, and was the first children's book to make it onto the *New York Times* Best-Seller List since E. B. White's *Charlotte's Web* in 1952. In 1999, after the publication of *Harry Potter and the Prisoner of Azkaban,* the Potter tales were numbers one, two, and three on the *Times* Best-Seller List. When *Harry Potter and the Goblet of Fire* came out in 2000, it sold an unbelievable 3 million copies in the United States in a single week. Children and their parents actually camped out overnight in front of bookstores to be sure to get their copies.

On December 18, 2001, *USA Today* announced that J. K. Rowling's Harry Potter books had made her the best-selling author in the world, surpassing the record previously held by mystery writer John Grisham. On that date, the four Harry Potter books in print were firmly entrenched on the best-seller lists, having been there for months and showing no signs of fatigue. They had been translated into more than 30 languages in more than 130 countries. The movie of the first novel, *Harry Potter and the Sorcerer's Stone,* was then opening to sell-out crowds around the world, and many children were standing in line to see it a third, fourth, or even fifth time. Stores all over the globe carried Harry Potter pop-up books, coloring books, trading cards, eyeglasses, watches, dolls, games, posters, magic wands, and other Potter-phernalia. Even the giant retailer Wal-Mart sells drapery material bearing the crests and names of Gryffindor, Hufflepuff, Slytherin, and Ravenclaw, the four student houses at Hogwarts School of Witchcraft and Wizardry. Author J. K. Rowling's agent in London, Christopher Little, has said he receives more than one hundred inquiries a day from people wanting to use Harry Potter's name and image to market various kinds of products.

All of this in spite of opposition from the Muggles—a word Harry's creator adapted and softened from "mug" (someone easily fooled) to designate the mundane, noncognoscenti populace that doesn't understand or sympathize with the world of wizardry—and can also well relate to the militant objectors purporting to represent the best interests of the Christian religion. Typical of these is a woman I know in Michigan who has forbidden her grandchildren to read the Potter books because of their "wicked" picture of "a world filled with wizards and goblins." She hasn't actually read the books, of course; but the word is out on the conservative grapevine that they are dangerous and unfit for public consumption. Many conservative Christian parents have led vigorous crusades to have the books banned from schools and libraries. James Dobson's Focus on the Family organization, one of the most powerful citizen groups in the United States, opposes the novels on its website. A massive protest in Columbia, South Carolina, orchestrated to coincide with one of Rowling's American book tours, argued that there is too much evil and darkness in the Potter stories, and that they promote witchcraft and wickedness. A minister in Alabama wrote to *USA Today* objecting to the attention the newspaper paid to the movie of *Harry Potter and the Sorcerer's Stone*. It was a nasty, evil film, he declared, despite the fact that he boasted of having neither seen the film nor read the novel from which it was made. Another minister, Pastor Jack Brock, of Christ Community Church in Alamogordo, New Mexico, had a "holy bonfire" on the Sunday after Christmas 2001, in which he publicly torched the Potter books, declaring them "an abomination to God and to me"!

There is a handsomely published book called *Harry Potter and the Bible,* by conservative Christian writer Richard Abanes, which assembles most of the pharisaical arguments against the Potter literature, blasting its supposed ties to the occult and to new-age philosophy, assailing Harry and his friends for the way they break rules, and insisting that "the books clearly present far too much moral subjectivity and patently unbiblical actions to be of any ethical value."[1] The author says *Harry Potter and the Goblet of Fire* "glamorizes dishonesty," and he criticizes Dumbledore for saying it is his belief that truth is (only) "generally" preferable to lies. He extols Percy Weasley as the kind of role model children should have, contends that scripture "tells us to behave in a way that is diametrically opposed to how Harry Potter" and his friends comport themselves, and accuses Rowling of catering to children's natural desire to be "grossed out" by unsavory descriptions of body fluids, crude jokes, and vulgar acts such as belching, vomiting, and "accidentally cursing."

Abanes also defends the conservative idolization of J. R. R. Tolkien and C. S. Lewis, insisting that their writings, which he dubs "mythopoetic," are not harmful to children because they create settings of complete imagination instead of interweaving fantasy and real life as Rowling does—something he is sure confuses Harry Potter fans into wanting to become witches and wizards. He praises Tolkien for his "masterful" tales and his "expansive imagination and brilliant mind," and extols Lewis because he "authored numerous books explaining and defending Christianity." Their Christian theology, he insists, is "veiled beneath various characters," while Rowling provides readers with "a *direct* link" to "current" paganism and the practice of witchcraft. There is indeed a witch in Lewis' Narnia stories, Abanes admits, "but she is evil and based on age-old and widely accepted symbols and illustrations of evil."[2] Apparently it is *attractive* witches who are out, for the conservative mind-set!

Perhaps nothing in *Harry Potter and the Bible* reveals the conservative way of thinking more than Abanes's advice to parents whose children must choose between remaining in a classroom where the teacher is reading from a Harry Potter story or suffering the embarrassment of asking to be excused. It may be better for them to remain in class, he concedes, than "being made to suffer the taunts of other children." But the parents should conduct "follow-up discussions" at home, and they might take the opportunity to introduce their children to "godly fantasy such as C. S. Lewis' Narnia series or J. R. R. Tolkien's books about Middle-Earth." The experience, more-over, "might open up witnessing opportunities for a child to share Christ's love with classmates."[3]

There is another, much more balanced, book by Connie Neal called *What's a Christian to Do with Harry Potter?* Disturbed by the controversy among Christians over the possible subversion of faith in the Potter stories, Neal takes a conciliatory approach, quoting both sides of the argument and pleading for a gentler, kinder, and more civil agreement to disagree. She admits that Rowling's narratives create *curiosity* about witchcraft among the young, and concedes that this can be disturbing to Christian parents. But she herself doesn't appear to regard the books as inherently evil, and suggests that they can even be employed to generate conversations with children that will prove helpful and enlightening. When a friend impugned Neal's faith for working on a book about Harry Potter, she says, she mollified the friend by telling her how she had "shared the gospel with a family friend by using the Harry Potter story as a redemptive analogy, and how he became a Christian shortly thereafter."[4]

One chapter in Neal's book is titled "What Would Jesus Do with Harry Potter?" It is an intriguing question—at least *I* found it so—and one the conservative religious mind will surely find central to any argument about the adolescent wizard. But Neal uses it craftily, suggesting that individual Christians will answer it according to their particular likes and prejudices, and that, because there can be no objective answer, it is important not to "turn it into a rhetorical question to tell someone else what Jesus would have *them* do."[5]

Let me be clear at the outset: I too am a Christian. In fact, I am an ordained clergyman and have in my lifetime ministered to six parishes, spanning the continent from Massachusetts to California. It has been my privilege to teach in four of the finest theological seminaries in the United States—the longest at Vanderbilt Divinity School in Nashville, where I was professor of Preaching, Worship, and Literature for fifteen years. I have spent the last seven summers as minister of a picturesque little church on Mackinac Island, Michigan, which is visited by thousands of worshipers from all over the world. I have written many books on the Bible, prayer, and various inspirational subjects. I have preached or lectured in many of the great churches of the world, as well as on campuses of seminaries and universities from Maine to California.

But in spite of all this, I confess to a very strong enthusiasm for J. K. Rowling's books (her name, incidentally, is Joanne Kathleen Rowling, and the last name is pronounced "rolling"). In fact, I could easily say, in the words of the old popular song, "I'm just wild about Harry." I remember when I first read *Harry Potter and the Sorcerer's Stone,* which I discovered on the shelves of the charming little public library on Mackinac Island. I found it hard to put down! When I absolutely had to, because of the press of duties, I kept thinking about it. The scenes scrolled through my mind as vividly as if I were watching a movie. No, it was better than that, it was a *virtual reality* movie. (After writing these lines, I was gratified to hear a youngster on CBS's *48 Hours* for February 3, 2002, say that, because Rowling tells her stories so well and in such vivid detail, he feels that he is *watching* them like a movie instead of *reading* them.) I *lived* the story of Harry Potter, the extraordinary young boy who, without a trace of personal hubris, becomes the primary nemesis of the evil Lord Voldemort and his nefarious Death Eater disciples.

Like the nine-year-old boy my son and his fiancée encountered in the theater, who was seeing *Harry Potter and the Sorcerer's Stone* for the fourth time and declared that he *was* Harry Potter, even lifting a shock of errant black hair to reveal a lightning-shaped mark on his forehead, I identified with Harry completely. I too had been a nerdy child, weak, bony, bespectacled, and completely unimpressive, with clumps of unruly hair. I never lived in a closet under the stairs, but my bedroom was in an unfinished attic space where I could look into the open roof trusses and got splinters in my bare feet from the rough, unfinished flooring. And I felt totally at the mercy of the selfish grown-ups and Dudley Dursleys in my life. When I read *Harry Potter and the Sorcerer's Stone,* I was whisked magically back to my boyhood and *became* Harry Potter, no question about it.

That, as I see it, is the essence of J. K. Rowling's skill as a storyteller. Of course she isn't C. S. Lewis or J. R. R. Tolkien, or, for that matter, Charles Williams, the third and lesser-known member of their coterie. (Am I permitted to offer a repressed "thank God!"?) She isn't male, she isn't an Oxford don, and she doesn't hang around the Eagle and the Child fetching beers for her companions and talking about English literature, medieval pageantry, and philosophies of linguistics. But she can tell a story with the best of them. Even Michael Dirda of *The Washington Post,* who worries that the Harry Potter books are keeping children from reading other things they should be reading, speaks of Rowling's "storytelling magic." Her narratives are transparent to the lives and actions of her characters. The glass is so clean, so absolutely devoid of smudges, that we look through it and are immediately caught up in the narrative. We duck when the owls begin flying everywhere, we fall in love with old Hagrid, whose hands are as big as the lids of dustbins and whose feet are like porpoises, and we suck in our breath when Harry gets on his Nimbus Two Thousand (later his Firebolt) and begins soaring like a miniature jet plane around the Hogwarts playing field.

Rowling's plotting is fantastic. Margo Jefferson said in *The New York Times* that "J. K. Rowling can plot as well as any thriller or television drama writer."[6] Small, apparently gratuitous details in the first novel show up with marvelous consequences in the later stories. And the writing! I have been a writer for years and years, and I find myself pausing to *envy* the way Rowling has described something, the crisp, efficient way her sentences propel the reader along, the sheer, beautiful economy of her prose. People are prone to think of books that receive so much hype and huckstering as potboilers—flimsy, airily fabricated stories written to please the masses and make a buck. The Harry Potter novels are anything but that. They will stand the test of decades—even centuries—as well contrived, carefully articulated stories with highly memorable characters.

And Rowling has this deliciously childlike appreciation for the simple way good and evil are juxtaposed in the world. Adults don't always see it. They have been trained not to look any-more—to pay more attention to so-called ordinary things like gas bills, frozen dinners, and NFL games. But children know better. They can still *feel* the existence of bad things in their universe—contrary spirits, hulking presences, the shadows of baleful intelligences all around them, threatening to do in the ordinary world, especially if it ever becomes conscious of them.

Maybe kids get it from reading comic books about super-heroes who are always fighting Armageddon-like battles. Or maybe, as Wordsworth suggested, they are really parents to the persons they will become, and know more about spiritual matters as infants than they will remember when they have grown up. Either way, they often have a sensitivity to impor-tant conflicts that their parents dismiss with a frown or a shrug, the way Ebenezer Scrooge dismissed the early signs of his approaching visitations as indigestion from eating a bit of beef or a bad potato. They know, even when their parents deny it, that there are more things in this world than the philosophers have dreamed of, and that these things portend both danger and excitement for youngsters willing to pay attention to them.

Thank God, I say, the Harry Potter stories will keep alive for a whole generation, even in this age of microchips and supertransistors, a sensitivity to the spiritual realities that lie at the heart of what it means to be human and inhabit a universe of competing energies such as the one in which we dwell. I, for one, salute J. K. Rowling and her glorious imagination. She is helping to save millions of youngsters from a sterile, passionless childhood, and from the grip of a video society that has long and fervently intended the demise of book publishing altogether. Someday, old and decrepit readers will arise and call her blessed, attributing to her and her alone their summons to the pleasures of the printed page, and a consequent lifetime of delight in books, first awakened by the Harry Potter series when they were young.

That is something a lot of Rowling's detractors miss, I fear, or simply don't care about—the way she has stimulated thousands of children to read who might never have read without her. The publication and distribution of her books has been nothing short of a miracle. To think that she was an out-of-work secretary and secondary-school teacher, lining up for her monthly assistance check, when she was first writing these brilliant stories! And then, once she came to the attention of an agent and a publisher, the books took off like an unquenchable fire, selling millions of copies in every language. It was as if the kindling had been laid in every hearth in the world, and suddenly the magic flame ignited it, so that the *whoof!* of it was astounding, was breathtaking—and we haven't begun to see the waning of the conflagration! Maybe that is what the detractors fear or envy—that their own notions of what people should be reading and talking about have not swept the globe with such speed and passion—indeed, haven't swept *anything* with speed and passion, even their own households, congregations, and communities.

Anyway—there are two basic premises in this book, *God,*

the Devil, and Harry Potter. The first is that the detractors are wrong and that the Potter stories, far from being "wicked" or "Satanic" (one widely quoted e-mail accuses Rowling of having written "an encyclopedia of Satanism"), are in fact narratives of robust faith and morality, entirely worthy of children's reading again and again, and even of becoming world classics that will be reprinted as long as there is a civilization. And the second premise is that much of that faith and morality is derived not only from the archetypes and legends of world literature, combined with Ms. Rowling's own fertile imagination, but from the wealth of Christian tradition that has spawned the author and her hero—a tradition that her detractors in their mean-spiritedness and narrow-mindedness (someone once spoke of an acquaintance so narrow-minded that he could peer through a keyhole with both eyes at the same time!) apparently do not know or else fail to appreciate.

Most of my attention shall be paid to the latter premise, as I attempt to suggest to the open-minded reader a few of the various ways in which the Potter mythology—for that is what it is, an expression of a *mythos* or worldview, regardless of critics like Abanes—is not only dependent on the Christian understanding of life and the universe *but actually grows out of that understanding and would have been unthinkable without it*.

It is true, as Elizabeth Schafer argues so well in her book *Exploring Harry Potter,* that the Potter stories are filled with classical allusions and shades of fairy tales, legends, and British history. J. K. Rowling took a double major in French and Classics at Exeter University, and both subjects have paid off handsomely in her stories. Hogwarts, for all its sounding like "hogwash," is a kind of Olympus, where Dumbledore is Zeus and Professor Minerva McGonagall is Athena. Hagrid is Orion, the wild hunter born of three gods' seed planted in the earth in the hide of a sacrificed bull, or Zagreus, the Cretan equivalent whose name sounds more like Hagrid and also represents the Titans. Professor Quirrell is Janus, the god with two faces, and the egotistical Gilderoy Lockhart is Narcissus, in love with his own image. The Forbidden Forest contains centaurs and unicorns. There are basilisks and hippogriffs and other mythical beasts in the stories. As Harry discovers in *Harry Potter and the Chamber of Secrets,* Hogwarts even has its own version of an underworld.

Dumbledore is also a kind of Merlin, who mentors Harry the way Merlin guided the young Arthur. Percy Weasley is Percival, King Arthur's loyal, punctilious knight. Merlin once disguised himself as a stag, the way James Potter, Harry's dad, was an Animagus who could transform himself into a stag. Harry quests for the Sorcerer's Stone the way Arthur sought the Holy Grail. As in Greek myths and Arthurian legends, the Potter stories are filled with special caves, stones, dragons, magical cloaks, and trees. The dreaded basilisk in *Harry Potter and the Chamber of Secrets* recalls the monster Grendel in *Beowulf.* Harry is a kind of Cinderella, who graduates from living under the stairs to being a prince among men. Hermione is put to sleep the way Snow White and Sleeping Beauty were. The living, dueling chessmen in the Hogwarts game are reminiscent of creatures Alice meets in Lewis Carroll's *Alice in Wonderland.*

Many of Rowling's characters and happenings are in fact quite polysemous—a word Dorothy Sayers employed to refer to the many layers of meaning in Dante's *Inferno*. Dumbledore's name, for example, is a British word for "bumblebee." It is equivalent to the Scottish *cockchafer*, which means "a May bug or beetle." The beetle was sacred in ancient Egyptian religion, which held that Khepera, or the scarab, rolled the sun into the sky each day the way a dung beetle rolls up little balls of dung in the sand. Blue or green beetles were enclosed in almost every sarcophagus. This becomes interesting when considered in reference to the opening scene of *Harry Potter and the Sorcerer's Stone*, where Professor McGonagall waits for Dumbledore outside the Dursley house in the form of a cat. The cat was also special in Egyptian mythology and was related to the moon because of the way moonlight shines in its phosphorescent eyes. It was believed that a female goddess named Bast took the form of a cat and sat with her foot on the head of the reptile Night, the enemy of the sun, until Khepera rolled the sun back into the sky at the start of the day. As Schafer says, the reason for the success of the Harry Potter series may well lie in J. K. Rowling's remarkable blending of archetypal patterns with the very imaginative symbols she herself has concocted!

But there are Christian references in the Potter novels as well, and a generally Christian structure to Rowling's understanding of the world. It is true, as Schafer notes, that "Harry does not attend church in either the Muggle or magical worlds, nor do any of his friends, teachers, or family."[7] It is also true that Halloween at Hogwarts bears little relation to All Saints'

Day, Christmas is a totally secular holiday (except for the singing of carols), and Easter "is referred to mostly as a way to note advancing time in the school calendar."[8] And yes, Harry and his friends, like ordinary children from any background, sometimes fudge the truth and break the rules to get their own way in a society controlled by grown-ups. Yet the world of Harry Potter would be inconceivable apart from the structures of Judeo-Christian theology and a very traditional Christian conceptualization of human existence and the way it should be approached by every follower of Jesus.

Beginning with Harry's miraculous survival as a baby (which is more like the survival of the infant Jesus than is usually noticed) and proceeding to discussions of the conflict between good and evil and the ethical considerations entailed by such a struggle, we shall in this book reflect at length on the possibility that Harry Potter, like Dostoevsky's Prince Myshkin, François Mauriac's Xavier Dartigelongue, and John Irving's Owen Meany, is a witting or unwitting Christ figure who actually battles the forces of darkness for the souls of the faithful and wins a place in readers' hearts because he so admirably conforms to our expectations for such a redemptive figure. If this possibility is true, and I believe it is, then what Ms. Rowling has furnished us, besides what the Brits call "a good read," and a whopping good one—maybe one of the best of all time, as millions of readers will attest—is a modern interpretation of the gospel, the wonderful news that "God was in Christ, reconciling the world to himself" and making sure that the goodness of creation would never be obliterated by the forces of darkness and evil.

MYSTERIOUS BIRTHS
AND MIRACULOUS CHILDHOODS

CHAP. 1.

T WAS LOGICAL for the producers to select *Harry Potter and the Sorcerer's Stone* as the first of J. K. Rowling's books to make into a movie, for it is the first of the novels and the one in which we are introduced to Harry as a baby, a foundling, actually, around whose delivery to his foster home occur several portentous and supernatural happenings. There is a downpour of shooting stars. Owls begin flying everywhere in the daytime, so that even the weather forecasters are talking about it. Inhabitants of the wizard world are standing around in little gatherings on street corners and outside pubs, so that the Muggles—the ordinary citizens—spotting them in their brilliantly colored cloaks wonder if it isn't "some stupid new fashion" or "some silly stunt." And one of the Hogwarts professors, Minerva McGonagall, parades around outside the Dursley home as a cat, who from time to time is seen studying a map to be sure she is at the right place.

Harry's parents have just been killed by Lord Voldemort, the dark wizard, whose name sounds a little like that of Vortigern, the evil king in the Arthurian legends who planned to kill Merlin, and may mean "the Flight of Death" (from the French *voler*, "to fly") or "the Will of Death" (from the Latin *volo*, "to will or be willing"). But Harry has miraculously survived. In fact, the Avada Kedavra, or Killing Curse, Voldemort pronounced on him actually backfired on the Dark Lord himself, nearly annihilating him, so that the good wizards of the world rejoice in the hope that he is gone for good.

Anyone familiar with the narratives surrounding the birth of Christ must surely feel a tingling of the skin at this point, recalling not only the acts of sympathetic magic in the universe when he was born but the wicked attempt to exterminate him and the godly presence he represented. While the angels heralded his arrival (like the mysterious appearance, in Harry's case, of the owls), the wicked King Herod sought the location of his birthplace, and, failing to secure it from the magi who discovered it by following a star, dispatched his soldiers to slay every Jewish male under two years of age. It was to escape this infanticide that the angel supposedly warned Jesus' father in a dream to "take the child and flee into Egypt."

The theme is, of course, not confined to early Christian legend. Moses, the leader of the ancient Hebrews, was also hidden at birth to save him from the wrath of an enemy. And as for Harry's power to resist Voldemort even at the age of one, there is a story about the Greek god Apollo in which he slays the giant Tityus for attacking Leto *immediately after he is born,* and another in which he kills a large serpent with bow and arrows while still in his mother's arms.

Harry is said to bear a peculiar reminder of his encounter with Voldemort—a jagged scar on his forehead similar to a bolt of lightning. At various times in Harry's life it will glow with an unearthly radiance and cause him excruciating pain when Voldemort is near or is contemplating some terribly evil deed. This is a nice touch, possibly more reminiscent of Batman films than anything in ancient mythology—Batman and Robin often had devices that warned them of the approach of crooks. It serves to identify Harry both as an extremely special person and as a survivor of his initial meeting with the powerful Dark Lord.

The mark of course becomes integral to Harry's character, the way Robert Graves in *The Greek Myths* says Odysseus' being gored by a boar when he was a young man led to his essential character. The Roman name for Odysseus, Ulysses, means "wounded thigh." And Marie-Louise von Franz begins her important work *Individuation in Fairy Tales* with the ancient Spanish narrative of "The White Parrot," which was originally Indian, then Persian, and tells about twin children, a boy and a girl, each born with a star on his or her forehead.

It is interesting that Rowling made Harry Potter's mark a lightning bolt. When the Torah describes the initial encounter between Moses and the divine, Moses asks God for his name so that he may cite it to the Egyptian pharaoh. God says it is Yahweh, which in most biblical versions is translated "I am who I am." Yahweh is actually represented in the Hebrew text by the tetragram YHWH, as traditional Hebrew uses no vowels. Among ancient Jews, it was an extraordinarily holy name, one never to be employed lightly. According to legend, it was spoken only once a year, on the high holy day of Yom Kippur, the Feast of the Atonement, and then only by the ritually purified high priest when he entered the Holy of Holies. And the thing that makes Rowling's choice of the lightning bolt for Harry's special mark from the encounter with Voldemort is that some Hebrew scholars believe the name YHWH originally meant *a flash of lightning*!

FAMILY CONNECTIONS

As in the case of Jesus, Harry's strongest connection to the supernatural comes from his mother's side. At least, it is her strong maternal love that saves him from Voldemort's power. His father is of course a blood wizard as well. But Harry's being taken by Dumbledore, McGonagall, and Hagrid to grow up in the Muggle household of the Dursleys is a potent reminder of his humanity as well, his relationship with ordinary mortals, or, in Christian terms, his incarnation in human flesh.

The Dursleys are caricaturish human beings. I suspect, in fact, that J. K. Rowling found the inspiration for Petunia Dursley, the sister of Harry's deceased mother, in the popular British TV comedy figure Hyacinth Bucket, the pretentious middle-class social climber who always insists that her name is actually pronounced *boo-KAY* and reminds people that her sister Violet lives in a mansion "with a Mercedes, a sauna, and room for a pony." Like Hyacinth, who tries desperately to conceal her relationship to her less affluent sisters Daisy and Rose, and especially to Daisy's neanderthalian husband, Onslow, Petunia (whose name is also "flowerful") doesn't want anybody to know about her controversial sister Lily (again, the name of a flower) and her husband, James, or that the skinny little boy with the unruly dark hair, so unlike her precious, chubby, blond-haired son, Dudley, is in any way related to her and her family.

The Dursleys, we are told, "had everything they wanted"; but they also had a secret they didn't want anybody to know, and that secret was Petunia's relation to a witch. The Dursleys and Potters hadn't seen each other in several years, and Petunia Dursley simply pretended to everyone that she didn't have a sister. Like Hyacinth Bucket, who shudders whenever she sees her sister Daisy and her family arriving in their backfiring old car, the Dursleys "shuddered to think what the neighbors would say if the Potters arrived in the street."[1] The Dursleys knew that the Potters had a young son, though they hadn't seen him, and this was another reason they wished to keep the Potters away: "they didn't want Dudley mixing with a child like that."[2]

When Harry shows up on the Dursleys' front stoop, they have to take him in because he is family. But he is treated like Cinderella, and given a closet under the stairway for his room. While his cousin Dudley gets birthday parties and incredible arrays of presents—at one birthday he counts only thirty-six presents and complains that he received thirty-eight the year before—Harry is barely tolerated in the Dursley household and is treated with undisguised contempt by both Dudley and his parents.

In spite of pious attitudes toward Jesus and the holy family, it should be recalled that he and his earthly family were not always on the best of terms. The one instance in which the Gospels speak of him as a youth occurs when he was taken to the temple at the age of twelve, probably for his bar mitzvah. It contains a chiding from his mother for an inconvenience he occasioned his parents. The parents had gone a day's journey away from Jerusalem when they discovered that their son was not in the caravan. Returning to Jerusalem and searching for three days, they eventually found him in the temple talking to the rabbis. His mother said, "Child, why have you treated us like this? Look, your father and I have been searching for you in great anxiety."[3]

Later, all three synoptic Gospels record an occasion when Jesus' mother and brothers came to a place where he was teaching, desiring to see him, and were left standing outside. Jesus reportedly said, "Who is my mother, and who are my brothers?" Then, pointing to his disciples, he answered his own question: "Here are my mother and my brothers! For whoever does the will of my Father in heaven is my brother and sister and mother."[4] It was a curious response, perhaps signaling a greater distance between him and his family than we usually imagine. Some scholars point to a preceding verse in the Markan passage as a possible explanation. There is a suggestion there that people were saying Jesus had "an unclean spirit"—that he was possessed by a demon and was ill or mad.

Having heard this, his mother and siblings might have come to fetch him home, and he possibly knew their motive in coming.

(Popular thought about Jesus and his mother is undoubtedly strengthened by the report in the Fourth Gospel that when Jesus was being crucified he consigned her to the care of John, the youngest apostle, saying that John was to consider her as his mother and she was to think of John as her son,[5] and also by many well-known artistic images of the pieta, or the grieving mother tenderly cradling her crucified son. But the Fourth Gospel is hardly the most reliable for historic detail, as much of it was contrived for rhetorical or theological reasons, and the pietas are obviously the products of later artistic imaginations.)

In addition to Harry's living with the Dursleys, there is, in the course of the Potter novels, another important reminder of his "earthly" connections. It has to do with the Sorting Hat's almost putting him into Slytherin House when he enters Hogwarts School of Witchcraft and Wizardry. The hat hesitates, then places him in Gryffindor House only because Harry has begged *not* to be put in Slytherin. Slytherin was founded by Salazar Slytherin (Rowling may have called him Salazar because Antonio de Oliveira Salazar was the name of the unpopular dictator of Portugal from 1932 to 1968, and she lived for a while in Portugal as a teacher), a dark wizard who spoke Parseltongue, or serpent language. It was also the house to which Voldemort belonged when he was a student at Hogwarts named Tom Riddle. Later, in *Harry Potter and the Chamber of Secrets*, Harry reflects on his having almost landed in Slytherin, and on the fact that he too speaks Parseltongue, like Voldemort. He even comes to the realization that his encounter with Voldemort when he was a baby left "a bit" of the Dark Lord in him. Dumbledore tells him, though, that he is *"very different"* from Voldemort because of the choices he has made about his life. It is our choosing that determines who we become.

When the young Jesus of Nazareth was baptized at the River Jordan by John the Baptist, it will be recalled, he was driven by the Spirit of God into the wilderness, where he spoke with the devil and endured three temptations to fall down and worship the evil one. Each time, he chose not to do so. Similarly, Harry converses with Voldemort in serpent language and rejects the Dark Lord's rule over his life. Jesus' choices determined his destiny as a redemptive figure and his eventual death on the cross. Harry's choices will lead him into direct conflict with Voldemort's purposes and, in *Harry Potter and the Goblet of Fire,* to the experience of the dreaded Cruciatus Curse, obviously so named because it causes its unfortunate victim to undergo a torment like that of a person being crucified.

The symbol of Gryffindor House is a lion. It is an image packed with many meanings, including the fact that the lion was the symbol of the tribe of Judah, to which Jesus belonged, and also of England. Richard the First of England, noted for his Christian faith and courage, was called Richard the Lion-Hearted. And in C. S. Lewis' Narnia tales, the Christ figure is the Great Lion, Aslan, son of the Emperor Beyond the Sea.

The emblem of Slytherin House, on the other hand, is the serpent, the traditional enemy of Judaism and Christianity. It is also the symbol of the Dark Lord, whose mark is a skull sprouting a tongue like a serpent, and whose "pet," in *Harry Potter and the Chamber of Secrets,* is the dreaded basilisk.

Harry Potter, like Jesus, has a foot in two realms. While he represents the lion, the noblest of beasts, he is also somehow related to the serpent, the lowliest of beasts and the enemy of all. But the allegiance he chooses—and Rowling gives great emphasis to the matter of choice—is to the lion, not the serpent. Like Jesus, he refuses to bow his knee to evil, and steadfastly pursues the higher path to righteousness and compassion. He is of the earth, earthy. But he is also destined for nobler things.

THE CINDERELLA MOTIF

It is perhaps the Cinderella motif itself—the beautiful person in disguise who will one day triumph over his or her surroundings—that immediately endears Harry Potter to J. K. Rowling's readers. As Professors Dumbledore and McGonagall discuss the death of Harry's parents while they wait outside the Dursleys' house for Hagrid to show up with the baby, they provide liberal hints of Harry's illustrious future. "He'll be famous—a legend," says Professor McGonagall, "—I wouldn't be surprised if today was known as Harry Potter Day in the future."[6] And later, when Hagrid has arrived and the baby is left on the doorstep, Rowling says, "Harry Potter rolled over inside his blankets without waking up. One small hand closed on the letter beside him and he slept on, not knowing he was special, not knowing he was famous."[7]

Professor McGonagall also unwittingly provides a clue to Harry's identity when she expresses astonishment at Albus Dumbledore's report that Voldemort was unable to kill Harry. "It's just astounding," she says, "but how in the name of heaven did Harry survive?"[8] It is all, of course, *in the name of heaven*—like the newborn Christ, Harry represents a supernal power at work in the world to defeat the spiritual wickedness that seeks to control everything.

Harry dwells beneath the stairway for the present, as Christ lived in a peasant home in Galilee. But one day the world will know, and, when it does, he will become the stuff of myth and legends!

Rowling may not have intended it, but her pairing of Professors Dumbledore and McGonagall at the Dursley home to see the baby safely deposited there is reminiscent of the aged couple in Luke's Gospel, Simeon and Anna, who see the baby Jesus when he is brought for presentation at the temple:

> Now there was a man in Jerusalem whose name was Simeon; this man was righteous and devout, looking forward to the consolation of Israel, and the Holy Spirit rested on him. It had been revealed to him by the Holy Spirit that he would not see death before he had seen the Lord's Messiah. Guided by the Spirit, Simeon came into the temple; and when the parents brought in the child Jesus, to do for him

what was customary under the law, Simeon took him in his arms and praised God, saying,

> *"Master, now you are dismissing your servant in peace,*
> *according to your word;*
> *for my eyes have seen your salvation,*
> *which you have prepared in the presence of all peoples,*
> *a light for revelation to the Gentiles*
> *and for glory to your people Israel."*

There was also a prophet, Anna the daughter of Phanuel, of the tribe of Asher. She was of a great age, having lived with her husband seven years after her marriage, then as a widow to the age of eight-four. She never left the temple but worshiped there with fasting and prayer night and day. At that moment she came [forward], and began to praise God and to speak about the child to all who were looking for the redemption of Jerusalem.[9]

When Dumbledore has carried the sleeping infant to the Dursleys' doorstep and laid him there, he, Professor McGonagall, and Hagrid stand looking at him for a minute. "Well," Dumbledore says finally, "that's that. We've no business staying here. We may as well go and join the celebrations."[10] Celebrations indeed! The sway of the Dark Lord is believed to be at an end. His little nemesis is sleeping peacefully. It seems a lot like the first Christmas Eve!

When the others have gone, Dumbledore produces his silver Put-Outer, with which he earlier doused the street lamps on Privet Drive, and clicks the lights back on again. Then he murmurs, "Good luck, Harry," swishes his cloak around him, and is gone.

It isn't quite a *Nunc dimittis*. But it doesn't miss by far!

CHILDISH POWERS

While the canonical Gospels are judiciously silent about Christ's doing miraculous things as a child—the miracles take place only in the world around him, in the appearance of angels and in the baby's surviving the threat of King Herod—there is no shortage in other places of legendary tales about his displays of childish powers. A. N. Wilson, in *Jesus: A Life,* refers to apocryphal Gospels that had him proclaiming his godhead, predicting the future of the world, and discoursing on the mysteries of creation—all while still in the cradle! He supposedly had the capacity to blink his eyes and bring the world to a stop, just as he had been present at the creation of everything.[11]

According to the Gospel of Thomas, a fourth-century Coptic Gospel, Jesus was two years old when he and his family arrived in Egypt. As they were passing through a field of corn or wheat and his childish hand reached out, he plucked some grain and chewed it. After that, the field yielded a number of bushels of wheat equal to the number of grains he had eaten. During the year that the holy family resided in Egypt, the infant Christ came upon some boys playing with a basin of water. He took a dried, salted fish, placed it in the basin, and ordered the salt to be expelled. The fish instantly came to life and swam about in the basin, striking fear into the other children, who ran home to tell their parents.

There is in the apocryphal book of James a famous story about Jesus when he was five. He made some clay sparrows as playthings on the Sabbath, and several of the adults, including Jesus' earthly father, Joseph, reprimanded him for making something on the day of rest. The child nonchalantly waved his arms and sent the sparrows flying into the air, telling them they would not meet death at anyone's hands.

Other stories in the Gospel of Thomas have the Savior-child making people blind or deaf for his amusement, or in some cases even killing them, only to restore them at his whim. Wilson mentions an Arabic Gospel that tells of a time when some children ran away, refusing to play with Jesus. He chased after them, and came into a woman's house where they were hiding in the cellar. He heard them moving about and asked the woman if they were in the cellar. She lied, saying no, those were only some goats. He replied, "Let the goats out." And when he opened the door to the cellar, she saw with horror that he had transformed the children into goats! Later, when the children's parents begged Mary and Joseph to get their son to restore their little ones, he happily did, and asked them once more to play with him. This time they were only too glad to do so![12]

Rowling attributes similar magical qualities to young Harry Potter. Once, when Petunia Dursley cut off most of his unruly hair, leaving only enough "to hide that horrible scar," Dudley laughed at Harry's near baldness, and Harry went to bed dreading school the next day, knowing the children would tease him mercilessly. But when he got up the following morning, his hair was exactly as it had been before his aunt cut it off!

When his Aunt Petunia attempted to put one of Dudley's old sweaters on him, which he found revolting, it grew smaller and smaller until she couldn't get it over his head, and she decided it must have shrunk in the wash. Another time, when Dudley's gang at school had been chasing Harry, Harry tried to leap over some trash cans to hide, and inexplicably found himself sitting atop the chimney over the school kitchen. Like Superman, he had been able to "leap tall buildings with a single bound"!

But Rowling's favorite story, and the one played up in the movie of *Harry Potter and the Sorcerer's Stone,* is the one about Harry in the reptile house at the zoo. It was on Dudley's birthday, and the Dursleys were taking Dudley and his friend Piers Polkiss to the zoo. They wanted to leave Harry behind, but had no one to leave him with and were afraid he would do something horrible to their house if they left him alone, so they ended up taking him with them. After lunch, Dudley headed for the reptile house, which was his favorite place at the zoo, and soon found the largest snake in the place. It was so huge that it could have wrapped itself around the Dursleys' car and compacted it into a trash can. But at the moment the snake was fast asleep. Dudley stood with his face pressed against the glass, wanting it to move. "Make it move," he whined to his father. But his father's rapping on the glass produced no effect, so they walked away.

Harry stood looking at the snake. As he did so, it slowly opened its eyes and raised its head until it was staring right at him. Then it *winked* at him! Harry winked back. The snake jerked its head toward Dudley and his father as if to say: I get that all the time. Harry agreed that it must be very annoying, and the snake nodded. When Harry asked where the snake came from, it pointed to the sign that said, "Boa Constrictor, Brazil." As they continued to converse in this strange manner, Dudley's friend Piers turned and saw them, and shouted at Dudley and his father to look, saying they wouldn't believe what the snake was doing!

Dudley came waddling back and pushed Harry away so he could have an unobstructed view. He and Piers were leaning close to the glass when suddenly it was no longer there and the huge snake came slithering out onto the floor beside them. They howled with fright, but it merely snapped at their heels and kept right on going. People in the reptile house were screaming and running every which way as it slithered along. As it passed Harry, still sitting on the floor where Dudley had pushed him, he heard it hiss, "Brazil, here I come. . . . Thanks, amigo."

The Dursleys weren't sure how, but they knew Harry was somehow to blame for what happened. So he had to endure the longest time he had ever spent confined to his cupboard under the stairs. When he got out, the school term was over and summer vacation had started.

As in the case of the apocryphal stories about Jesus, the main purpose served by these stories about Harry is to underline his fantastic powers and foreshadow the much more important things he will do in the future. He might live among ordinary people, the Muggles, but he himself is clearly much more than ordinary.

THE UNKNOWN YEARS

Much has been made, over the centuries, of Jesus' so-called unknown years, the long span of time in which nothing appears to be known about him, except, of course, for the apocryphal stories. It is believed that he was about thirty years old when he began his public ministry, appearing to John the Baptist at the River Jordan and asking to be baptized, following which he entered the wilderness for forty days and nights and underwent the ritual of the three great temptations. But, with the lone exception of Luke's tale about his lingering in the temple with the rabbis when he was twelve, there is no word about his life from the time the family returned from Egypt, presumably when he was two or three, until that dramatic appearance some twenty-seven years later.

There are, of course, many tales and legends about Jesus during this interim period, one of which involved a boyhood visit to England. The poet William Blake mentions the story in his long poem "Jerusalem." Apparently it was widely held that Joseph of Arimathea, not the father of Jesus but the wealthy man mentioned in the Gospels as the owner of the tomb where Jesus was buried, had made trips to England as a tin merchant. On one of these trips, he brought along the young Jesus and his mother, and they landed at St. Michel's Mount, off the coast of southwest England. After Jesus' death, Joseph was rumored to have brought the Holy Grail, the goblet from which Jesus and the disciples drank at the Last Supper, to Glastonbury, in Somerset, where he buried it. There was even a wrinkle in the story that said the original church at Glastonbury had been built by Jesus as a monument to his mother when he was a teenager.

There are, certainly, great lapses of time in Harry Potter's life when we are not told what was happening, but it would not have served J. K. Rowling's purposes to skip over his childhood and present him to her audience as an adult. She began the Harry Potter series, after all, as a collection of stories designed for and about children—even though she has confessed that she wrote them for adults as well. What we get, instead, after a rather brief description of Harry's infancy and a little of his unpleasant existence with his Dursley relations, is the narrative of the incredible barrage of mail about Harry's enrollment at Hogwarts School and then, when he is eleven years old, his actual departure from the Dursley household to take up life as a student at Hogwarts.

The mail barrage is a very curious episode, pivoting on Uncle Vernon's refusal to allow Harry to have the letters that arrive addressed to him. The letters come thicker and thicker, necessitating Vernon's nailing up the mail slot to keep them out of the house and eventually leading him to take the family to a broken-down house on a barren island off the coast where there is no mail service. And there, in the middle of a terrifically stormy night, the giant gamekeeper Hagrid appears, bends the gun Vernon waves at him into a pretzel, informs Harry that he's a wizard, and presents him with a letter stating that he has been accepted as a student at Hogwarts School of Witchcraft and Wizardry, thus marking the end of Harry's period of waiting.

Still, there is one similarity to Christ's coming of age and being baptized by John at the start of his ministry. It was at this point that Jesus' being chosen by God was first made plain, when a *bat qôl,* or "daughter of a voice," spoke out of heaven to say, "This is my beloved Son, in whom I am well pleased."

Harry has not known, until Hagrid appears on the island with the letter, that he is a wizard or that he has any future other than an extension of the same miserable life he has been leading under the Dursleys' stairway. Hagrid becomes furious with the Dursleys for having hidden the letter Albus Dumbledore left with the child on their doorstep and kept from him the information that his parents were wizards and were killed by Voldemort. They had told him, in fact, that his parents died in a car crash. To which Hagrid exploded, "Car crash! How could a car crash kill Lily an' James Potter? It's an outrage! A scandal! Harry Potter not knowin' his own story when every kid in our world knows his name!"[13]

As Hagrid recounts Voldemort's killing of Harry's parents and attempting to slay Harry in the same way, only to be unsuccessful and managing merely to leave the scar made by his powerful curse, Harry remembers clearly what he had not been able to remember well before—a blinding flash of green light and "a high, cold, cruel laugh." He asks Hagrid what happened to Voldemort. Hagrid says that nobody knows. Some wizards speculate that he had enough humanity left in him to die. Others say no, he is out there somewhere, merely biding his time before he strikes again. Whatever happened, he met his match in Harry, even though Harry was only a baby.

Hagrid regards Harry with "warmth and respect" approaching adoration. But Harry is so stunned by the announcement that he is a wizard that he can't really take it in. His whole life, practically, has been spent with the Dursleys. Dudley has battered him regularly, and Aunt Petunia and Uncle Vernon have treated him like an outcast whom they could barely tolerate in their home. If he is really a wizard, then why haven't they turned into ugly toads every time they've locked him in the closet under the stairs? It didn't make sense. When he says this to Hagrid, Hagrid only laughs. And, after a scuffle in which he turns Vernon Dursley into a pig, Hagrid carries Harry off to London to get him ready to go to Hogwarts.

Devoted Christians, prone to read an imperialist theology back into all the details of Jesus' biography in the Gospels, think of his wilderness temptations—to turn stones into bread, to worship the devil in exchange for a kingdom, and to throw himself down from the pinnacle of the temple to test whether God would not bear him up[14]—as evidences of his strength and determination as the Savior of the world. But is it possible, if only barely, that it was the other way around—that instead of being confident of himself as the chosen of God, he could not really believe it any more than Harry could believe he was a wizard, and went into the wilderness as an attempt to clear his head and get his thinking straight? Was he only *testing* the voice that had pronounced him the Son of God, the way Harry tested Hagrid's announcement that he was famous in the wizard world and that everybody in that world was expecting great things of him?

In both cases—Jesus' and Harry's—they must face what they are about in the world, namely, that they are instrumental in the age-old conflict between good and evil powers, and are about to embark upon remarkable careers filled with good works, formidable opposition, and an eventual struggle to the death with the wicked force seeking their destruction. And it is to the similarities of those careers that we must now turn.

THE STRUGGLE
BETWEEN GOOD AND EVIL

CHAP. 2.

HERE HAS BEEN only one great plot engine for all fiction since the coming of Christ, and that is the struggle of good to overcome evil. Before Christ, in the eras of great Hellenistic and Roman literature, this was not true. There was struggle in *The Iliad, The Odyssey,* and *The Aeneid,* but it was not about the conflict between good and evil; this essential ingredient in all great Western literature (and even many of the lesser writings) is derived from Hebrew and Christian theology, and especially the Gospels, with their portrayal of the battle between Christ and the forces of darkness. Today, whether we are reading Agatha Christie, Tom Clancy, John Grisham, P. D. James, Barbara Delinsky, Toni Morrison, or Barbara Kingsolver, we expect our interest to be aroused and maintained by an honest-to-goodness contest mimicking that of Christ and his mortal enemies.

J. K. Rowling does not disappoint us. The major plot

device in the entire Harry Potter saga is the dangerous, abiding menace of the Dark Side, as we met it in *Harry Potter and the Sorcerer's Stone,* which is forever attempting, out of its evil, malicious nature, to annihilate the good in the world. We have barely turned a page of the first Potter novel when we learn of the dastardly attack of Voldemort—whose very name is so terrible that most wizards refuse to speak it—on Harry's family, and that Harry wears, throughout the saga, the jagged mark on his forehead that is the residue of that fateful encounter. As surely as Sherlock Holmes was destined to battle the villainous Moriarty, Harry is bound to mortal conflict with the great Death Will, whose lesser adumbrations, Draco Malfoy, his father, Lucius, and Professor Quirrell, are only minions in his kingdom of darkness and hate.

Briefly, here is the story of the first novel: Harry's parents have been killed by Voldemort, the primal villain. When Harry goes to Hogwarts, the wizardry school, he learns that a Sorcerer's Stone created by one Nicolas Flamel (a real historical character, by the way) has been moved from Gringotts Bank, where Harry's parents left the money he inherited, to a secret location in the school where it is guarded by Hagrid's great three-headed dog named Fluffy (which sounds much nicer than Cerberus). The stone has two incredible qualities: It can create all the gold its possessor desires and provide its owner with the Elixir of Life—the possibility of never dying. Harry and his friends Ron and Hermione suspect Professor Snape, who is an unpleasant wizard and seems to have it in for Harry, of plotting to steal the Stone.

One night Harry, Ron, Hermione, Neville Longbottom,

and Draco Malfoy are being punished for being caught in an off-limits area after hours. Their punishment consists of being led by Hagrid into the Forbidden Forest, which is a frightening experience, and a dangerous one, because something in the forest has been killing unicorns. The "something" turns out to be Voldemort, who is drinking unicorn blood to maintain his strength until he can get his hands on the Sorcerer's Stone. He and Harry almost have an encounter there, but Harry is saved by a centaur named Firenze, who frightens off Voldemort and carries Harry back to Hagrid and the others.

Learning that Professor Dumbledore has been lured to London by a false message, Harry, Ron, and Hermione rush to the Stone's hiding place, hoping to save it. After a gauntlet of obstacles, Harry reaches the hiding place, and finds, not Professor Snape, but the stuttering Professor Quirrell. Quirrell is in the service of Voldemort, and it was he who was drinking the unicorn blood, in Voldemort's behalf. When Quirrell removes from his head the turban he always wears, Harry sees that the back of his head is occupied by Voldemort's face.

Voldemort must have the Sorcerer's Stone in order to become strong again. But he and Quirrell have not been able to find it. The Mirror of Erised, which is supposed to reveal what the viewer wishes to see, is there. Quirrell has been staring at it, trying to read the location of the Stone. Voldemort tells him to have Harry look into the mirror; perhaps it will yield its secret to him. When Harry looks, he feels the Stone slipping magically into his pocket. Voldemort orders Quirrell to kill Harry, but when Quirrell touches him, his hands are sorely burned. Harry grasps Quirrell and holds him tightly, thinking it the only way to survive. He passes out, supposing he has lost the battle. But he awakens in the hospital, where Dumbledore sits by his side and explains everything. It was Harry's mother's love that was still protecting him when Quirrell tried to harm him.

Dumbledore, having arrived in London and realized the call was a hoax, rushed back in time to intervene and save Harry. Quirrell died, but Voldemort escaped. And Dumbledore, in conference with his old friend Nicolas Flamel, decided to destroy the Stone so it would no longer be a temptation.

There are several subplots to the story, of course, including the friendship of Harry with Ron, Hermione, and Neville; the young wizards' efforts to master curses, potions, and simple magic; the rivalry between Harry and Draco Malfoy; the softness of Hagrid's heart, especially for Harry, Fluffy, and a fledgling dragon named Norbert; and the yearlong battle among the four student houses, Gryffindor, Hufflepuff, Ravenclaw, and Slytherin, for the prestigious house cup awarded at the end of the last term. But the master plot, the one underlying the entire novel, is the critical struggle between good and evil—the one in which Harry, the often unwitting Christ figure, aided by Professor Dumbledore, who is a kind of God the Father watching just offstage most of the time, ends by defeating Voldemort, the personification of all that is wicked and unholy.

(Is it only an accident of Rowling's narrative art that Harry is in a coma for three days following his supreme exertion with Quirrell and Voldemort, and then returns to consciousness with Dumbledore looking over him and answering all his questions about what has happened? Or is this a subtle allusion to the three days Christ was in the grave following his death on the cross and preceding his resurrection?)

It is unfortunate that fundamentalist Christians have been put off Rowling's novels by all the talk of witches, goblins, spells, incantations, potions, dragons, invisible capes, and magic stones, and reacted by branding such harmless devices as "Satanic" and "anti-Christian"; for the story Rowling tells, again and again, is the one so basic to Christian belief, of a cosmic battleground on which the servants of God are continuously engaged in mortal combat with the forces of evil, and of the way characters define themselves and their eternal fate by identifying with one or the other of these eternal armies.

THE MIXED FIELD

What is the righteous hero to do in a world where evil, like the Devil's Snare plant guarding the way to the Sorcerer's Stone, is waiting to entrap the unwary victim? Can the evil be uprooted, burned, destroyed? Not in this world, unfortunately. That is the theme of a parable told by Jesus in the Gospel of Matthew:

> The kingdom of heaven may be compared to someone who sowed good seed in his field; but while everybody was asleep, an enemy came and sowed weeds among the wheat, and then went away. So when the plants came up and bore

grain, then the weeds appeared as well. And the slaves of the householder came and said to him, "Master, did you not sow good seed in your field? Where, then, did these weeds come from?" He answered, "An enemy has done this." The slaves said to him, "Then do you want us to go and gather them?" But he replied, "No; for in gathering the weeds you would uproot the wheat along with them. Let both of them grow together until the harvest; and at harvest time I will tell the reapers, 'Collect the weeds first and bind them in bundles to be burned, but gather the wheat into my barn.' "[1]

Good and evil are a complicated business. Good sometimes looks like evil, as in the case of Professor Snape, whose dislike of Harry makes Harry and his friends think Snape is on Voldemort's side; and evil often masquerades as good, as it does in the case of the stuttering Professor Quirrell. And weak persons, like young Ginny Weasley in *Harry Potter and the Chamber of Secrets*, sometimes vacillate between the two and, for one reason or another, such as ambition or greed or love, permit themselves to be drawn into evil's web and employed by it to achieve its own ends.

Jesus' parable of the field makes it clear that in this world the two are really inextricable. The complete destruction and eradication of evil would destroy much that is good as well. So good people must be prepared to deal with evil over the long haul. They must learn patience and wisdom, and equip themselves to exist in a land where the wicked may strike at any moment, and from the most unexpected quarters.

The fatherly Dumbledore understands this, and tries to explain it to Harry when he sits by Harry's bed in the hospital. Harry already suspects it, and asks if Voldemort won't make another appearance sometime, some way: "I mean, he hasn't gone, has he?"

> "No, Harry, he has not [says Dumbledore]. He is still out there somewhere, perhaps looking for another body to share . . . not being truly alive, he cannot be killed. He left Quirrell to die; he shows just as little mercy to his followers as his enemies. Nevertheless, Harry, while you may only have delayed his return to power, it will merely take someone else who is prepared to fight what seems a losing battle next time—and if he is delayed again, and again, why, he may never return to power."[2]

Dumbledore's statement that Voldemort isn't truly alive is interesting, and is consistent with Voldemort's name, "Flight of Death" or "Will of Death." It is as if he is a condition or a disease rather than a real person. He is a negative value corrupting the world, like the weeds in Jesus' story. And he will not be eradicated until the world itself comes to an end. He *seems* to be eliminated at the end of *Harry Potter and the Chamber of Secrets*, after his third attempt on Harry's life; but the reader cannot doubt that he will be back again in another guise. And the reader's fears are of course confirmed by his strong resuscitation in *Harry Potter and the Goblet of Fire*.

When we reflect on Jesus' encounters with evil in the

Gospels, they boil down basically to four. The first was in his infancy, when Herod attempted to get rid of him by slaying all males under two years old. The second was in the wilderness temptations immediately following his baptism and preceding his ministry. The third was in all his niggling confrontations with the Pharisees and Sadducees throughout his ministry—people he called evil because of their hypocrisy, pretending to be righteous when they were not. The fourth and final encounter was at his capture and crucifixion by the Romans, when darkness spread over all the earth at midday, symbolizing the momentary flickering of the Light that had come into the world at his birth.

Harry Potter experiences the first type of encounter when Voldemort attempts to kill him at birth, and the fourth in the fight over the Sorcerer's Stone, in the chamber of secrets, and in the cemetery at the climax of *Harry Potter and the Goblet of Fire*. A case might be made for his undergoing the second type of encounter, the temptation, as well—especially in the summer he spends with the Dursleys in *Harry Potter and the Chamber of Secrets,* when he is sorely tempted to use his magic but faithfully restrains himself because he is not supposed to use it away from the Hogwarts campus. But it is the third type of encounter—the small, everyday confrontations with minions of evil—that constitutes the bulk of the novels, just as it accounts for most of the narratives in the Gospels. This is the stuff of daily life—the slow, grinding struggle against evil that consumes us all our days, often undramatically, always wearing, and eventually flowing, like rivers to the sea, into the pure concentration of evil that exists as an onto-logical threat to all civilization.

The Voldemorts, Lucius Malfoys, and Barty Crouches add high drama to Harry's tales. But it is the Draco Malfoys and Professor Snapeses who constitute the major drain on his energy, because they are so relentlessly there, so regularly in his face, so consistently teasing, jealous, insulting, and malicious in their dealings. Just as the Pharisees and Sadducees were always needling Jesus, probing for his weaknesses and undermining him with other people, the Malfoys and Snapeses are the daily pain of a good and idealistic person like Harry.

What J. K. Rowling sees, and faithfully conveys in her narratives straight out of her Christian catechism, is the way people like Malfoy and his friends Goyle and Crabbe *lend themselves* to evil and, in the end, whether through weakness or greed or personal ambition, become part of the corrosive force of evil in the world. They are little fish, hardly worthy of being called wicked in and of themselves. But they are part of the circulating evil in the world that contaminates the atmosphere for others and thereby spoils what might otherwise be a kind of paradise. They are the unwanted weeds that cannot be uprooted without destroying people and things around them, and as such they are a judgment upon themselves.

A CONTINUING BATTLE

Each of the Harry Potter books is an episode in the constant struggle with evil. Harry doesn't seek evil. It simply finds him, in the way evil has of zeroing in on those who represent goodness and innocence in the world. He would like nothing better than to play Quidditch, enjoy his friends, and get on with his life. But Voldemort's failure to kill him when he was an infant has made him famous as a resister of evil, and, just as the old Western films often turned on the motif of the wicked gunslinger who wanted his chance to gun down some mild-mannered hero who was known for his prowess with a pistol, Voldemort and his followers keep circling and returning to Harry, wanting to destroy the very symbol of their opposition.

Harry Potter and the Chamber of Secrets is the chronicle of Harry's twelfth year on earth, and is, for the first hundred pages or so, a very funny book, with lots of humorous characters and incidents. We meet Dobby, for example, the self-flagellating little house-elf (Elizabeth Schafer calls him a kind of leprechaun) who comes to the Dursley home to warn Harry not to return to Hogwarts, and we follow Harry to the Weasley home, known as the Burrow, which is the first wizard house Harry has ever seen, filled with strange artifacts and fascinating witching books. When Harry and the Weasleys travel to Diagon Alley, where the Hogwarts students purchase their school supplies, they go by Floo powder, and Harry gets off at the wrong grate and winds up instead in nefarious Knockturn

Alley. And when, for an unknown reason, Harry and Ron Weasley can't enter the usual way into track nine and three-quarters at King's Cross Station, they fly to Hogwarts in Mr. Weasley's enchanted old Ford Anglia, a car extremely reminiscent of Herbie, the Walt Disney VW with an attitude. (Rowling says the real prototype was a turquoise Ford Anglia that belonged to her high school chum, Sean Harris.) The car develops trouble near Hogwarts and crashes into the Whomping Willow Tree at the edge of the Forbidden Forest, which nearly beats both them and the car to death. It is all lots of fun, and the reader begins to wonder if Rowling has turned entertainer in her second novel and is no longer concerned about the great existential and ontological conflict that marked the first one.

But then hints begin to coalesce, confirming the prediction of the house-elf Dobby that something terrible is in the offing. Draco Malfoy has become the Seeker on the Slytherin Quidditch team, because his father, Lucius Malfoy—whose first name links him with Lucifer, the enemy of God—bought the entire team new Nimbus Two Thousand and One broomsticks. Draco calls Harry's friend Hermione a *Mudblood*—an opprobrious name for wizards born of Muggle parents. Harry begins hearing a strange voice in the hall—"a voice of breath-taking, ice-cold venom." It says, "Come . . . come to me . . . Let me rip you . . . Let me tear you . . . Let me kill you. . . ."

All these things are intertwined. Lucius Malfoy, like Salazar Slytherin, for whom Slytherin House was named, wants to eliminate all students who are either Mudbloods or semi-Mudbloods. A series of mysterious petrifications begins to occur—first a cat, then some students—and it is clear that they are somehow connected with a monster that lives in a secret chamber created years ago by Salazar Slytherin somewhere in the bowels of Hogwarts.

In a women's bathroom presided over by a ghost named Moaning Myrtle, Harry finds a diary that once belonged to T. M. Riddle, a student at the school fifty years ago. Although it is blank, Harry discovers that if he speaks to it, it will talk back to him. And, on the page for June 13, he watches as the little square for that date becomes a miniature TV screen. Putting his eye to the space, Harry watches as his friend Hagrid, at that time a student at Hogwarts, is accused of releasing the monster, and is expelled from school.

As fear stalks Hogwarts, Lucius Malfoy shows up with an order from the board of governors for Albus Dumbledore to step down from the headmaster's job. At the same time, Hagrid is taken away to Azkaban, the wizard prison, on suspicion that he has let the monster out of the chamber again.

Harry's friend Hermione is petrified by the monster. When Harry and Ron visit her lifeless body in the infirmary, Harry notices a piece of paper clutched in one of her rigid hands. Prying it out and reading it, he discovers that it is a page from a book about the deadly basilisk, legendary King of Serpents. Suddenly everything becomes clear to Harry: The mysterious voice he has been hearing in the corridors is a serpent's voice. He could hear it, while others couldn't, because he speaks Parseltongue—snake language—his means of communicating with the serpent at the reptile house in *Harry Potter and the Sorcerer's Stone*.

But where is the basilisk? At the end of the page in Hermione's hand, she has scribbled the word *pipes*. Harry remembers the toilet, and realizes that Moaning Myrtle, the ghost, was killed by the basilisk. Perhaps the monster dwells in the pipes beneath the bathroom, and Myrtle lives there because that is where she was murdered. Just as Harry is coming to this conclusion, the stakes are raised: Ginny Weasley, Ron's little sister, has been abducted by the monster and taken to the chamber. With Ron and Professor Lockhart, Harry hurries to the bathroom and says in Parseltongue, "Open up!" A sink begins to writhe and shift, and soon opens to reveal a large pipe. "I'm going down there," announces Harry, in an action reminiscent of the *descensus ad inferos* of Jesus.

The long trip through a dark tube ends in the chamber miles below the school. There Harry finds Ginny, petrified, and a tall, dark-haired boy standing near her, who identifies himself as Tom Riddle, the owner of the diary. Harry asks if he is a ghost. He says he is a "memory." Harry says they must get out before the basilisk returns. Tom says it won't come until it is called. Tom is not merely Tom Riddle; he is Lord Voldemort, Harry's archenemy, and he has been scheming to get Harry alone in order to kill him. He and Tom Riddle, he says, have been one from the first—the name Tom Marvolo Riddle is an anagram of "I Am Lord Voldemort"—and brags that he is the greatest sorcerer in the world.

He isn't, says Harry; Albus Dumbledore is.

Voldemort becomes angry.

Music begins to erupt in the chamber—eerie, unearthly music. Suddenly a majestic bird the size of a swan appears, with fiery red feathers and golden tail and talons. It is Albus Dumbledore's phoenix, named Fawkes (for Guy Fawkes, the gunpowder plot conspirator, whose day is celebrated with bonfires in England each November fifth), which has just been reborn from its ashes and is extremely powerful. It has come to help Harry because of his faithfulness to Dumbledore.

Voldemort orders the monster to appear and kill Harry. The chamber wall parts and the giant basilisk emerges, its yellow eyes flashing ominously. Harry keeps his eyes shut so that he won't be paralyzed by its gaze. He hears sounds of a tremendous thrashing. When he dares to peek, he sees that the phoenix has pecked out both of the basilisk's eyes. Voldemort commands the monster to *smell* the boy and kill him. But Harry has become miraculously armed with a sword, and, like St. George, he plunges it into the serpent's mouth. He is wounded in the act of doing this, and appears to be dying from a great poisonous fang embedded in his arm. The phoenix hovers over him, weeping tears into the wound, and it is miraculously healed. Outraged, Voldemort raises his wand to destroy Harry. But the phoenix flies over Harry's head and drops the diary in his lap. Harry plunges the basilisk's fang into the heart of the diary, and Voldemort screams, collapses, twists on the floor, and—disappears!

This is all highly fanciful, of course, but no more so than

the great drama in the book of Revelation when God's angels bind Satan and cast him into the lake of everlasting fire. Eschatological battles require apocalyptic language and images. They cannot be described by ordinary pictures. Something far more vivid and outsize is necessary. Consider this passage from Revelation, in which Satan is expelled from heaven:

> And war broke out in heaven; Michael and his angels fought against the dragon. The dragon and his angels fought back, but they were defeated, and there was no longer any place for them in heaven. The great dragon was thrown down, that ancient serpent, who is called the Devil and Satan, the deceiver of the whole world—he was thrown down to the earth, and his angels were thrown down with him. . . .
>
> So when the dragon saw that he had been thrown down to the earth, he pursued the woman who had given birth to the male child. But the woman was given the two wings of the great eagle, so that she could fly from the serpent into the wilderness, to her place where she is nourished for a time, and times, and half a time. Then from his mouth the serpent poured water like a river after the woman, to sweep her away with the flood. But the earth came to the help of the woman; it opened its mouth and swallowed the river that the dragon had poured from his mouth. Then the dragon was angry with the woman, and went off to make war on the rest of her children, those who keep the commandments of God and hold the testimony of Jesus.[3]

The sweep and the imagery are not that different from those employed by Rowling. In fact, there can be little doubt where Rowling got the idea of the King of Serpents for her story, whether she did so consciously or unconsciously.

And if it is true, as I earlier suggested, that Albus Dumbledore is a kind of heavenly Father watching over Harry Potter as a Christ figure (why else did he stand outside the Dursleys' home that night when Hagrid arrived with the baby?), is it not also possible that Dumbledore's great phoenix somehow symbolizes the Holy Spirit that often came and ministered to Jesus during his years of ministry? Rowling's description suggests as much. The phoenix arrives with the sound of "unearthly" music and is seen first in flames that erupt at the top of a pillar. The music grows louder and louder, until it lifts the hair on Harry's head and makes his heart feel as though it is swelling to twice its size. Then the bird shows itself with magnificent crimson plumage and glittering, golden tail feathers. When the disciples of Jesus were gathered on Pentecost, following his crucifixion and resurrection, they first heard "a sound like the rush of a violent wind," which filled the entire house where they were sitting. Then "divided tongues, as of fire, appeared among them."[4] Perhaps the similarities are only coincidental—if anything in this world really is.

Afterward, when Harry and Dumbledore are reviewing what has occurred, Dumbledore hands Harry the bloodstained silver sword with which he dispatched the basilisk. Harry turns it over, its great rubies blazing in the firelight. And then he sees the name engraved on the hilt: GODRIC GRYFFINDOR.

Godric is a great old Anglo-Saxon name. But is its meaning—"God-rich"—an accident?

Will this be the end of Voldemort? Has Harry truly vanquished him for good? Not unless the world has come to an end. The wheat and the weeds must continue to grow together. Lucius Malfoy is dismissed from the school's board of governors, and his son Draco has to stop swaggering about as if he owned Hogwarts. Of course, Dumbledore returns in glory, and Hagrid comes back to his gamekeeper's cottage at the edge of the Forbidden Forest, to be made Professor of the Care of Magical Creatures in the next novel. Harry tricks Lucius Malfoy into freeing Dobby, his house-elf. There is a great celebration for the end of term, and Harry thinks he's never been happier.

But we know the lull in hostilities is only temporary. Evil has been defeated once again, but not permanently. There will be another story, and another battle.

SAME WAR, ANOTHER BATTLE

The whole creation, wrote St. Paul, "waits with eager longing for the revealing of the children of God," so that it too "will be set free from its bondage to decay."[5] For the Jews and early Christians, the Creation meant especially the nonhuman living things in the world—birds, animals, fish, reptiles, and even insects. The Bible is filled with references to them, from the serpent in the Garden of Eden (and in stories about Moses and Jesus) to the doves, lambs, and oxen of the sacrificial system, the great beasts of Job's vision (probably a hippopotamus, a crocodile, and a whale), the lion that was the symbol of Judah, the ram and the goat of Daniel's apocalyptic passion, the donkey ridden by Zion's king in the prophecy of Zechariah (and later by Jesus in the Triumphal Entry), and the leopard, horses, dragons, and of course the Lamb in the book of Revelation.

Birds and animals figure prominently in Rowling's work as well. Owls, cats, dragons, unicorns, and hippogriffs, like their biblical predecessors, are a reminder of the connection between the natural world and the spiritual world, and help to heighten the sense that a cosmic battle is taking place. In none of the novels is this more true than in *The Prisoner of Azkaban,* where several of the characters themselves are Animagi, able to transfigure themselves into animals at will.

Azkaban is the wizards' equivalent of Alcatraz, a rocklike prison surrounded by water, from which escape is almost impossible. The prisoners are guarded by *dementors,* ghoulish beings who kiss their unfortunate inmates and suck the minds or souls out of them. In *The Odyssey,* Mentor acts as a wise and faithful counselor, helping his friends Odysseus and Telemachus to make up their minds. In *The Prisoner of Azkaban,* it is the other way around: The dementors *take away* people's minds.

One renowned prisoner, however, has been at Azkaban twelve years without losing his soul to the dementors. He is Sirius Black, named for the Dog Star, who can transform himself into a large black dog, and is reputed to have betrayed Harry Potter's parents to Voldemort. We learn early in the novel that Black has escaped from Azkaban and is on his way to Hogwarts, apparently to kill Harry. The entire novel turns on this threat of harm to Harry, whose father, we learn, was also an Animagus.

In the complicated denouement, which follows the usual array of delightful sideplots, fascinating gadgets, and thrilling Quidditch matches, we learn that James Potter had three close friends at Hogwarts: Sirius Black, Remus Lupin, and Peter Pettigrew. Lupin, now a professor at Hogwarts, is a werewolf (his name means "wolf," and Remus was one of the twins suckled by a wolf in Roman legend). James, Sirius, and Peter mastered the skill of transfiguration in order to accompany Lupin when he turned into a werewolf and see that he came to no harm. James became a stag, Sirius a dog, and Peter a rat. Their nicknames were, respectively, Prongs, Padfoot, and Wormtail.

At the climax of the story, as the dementors are closing in on Sirius, Harry and his friends make the discovery that it was Peter Pettigrew, not Sirius, who betrayed Harry's parents. When Sirius afterward hunted Pettigrew down on the streets of London, Pettigrew attempted to blast him with a curse, striking and killing twelve Muggles in the vicinity. Then Pettigrew changed into a rat and slipped away, leaving Sirius to be apprehended for the crime. The dementors had been unable to rob Sirius of his soul because he was innocent—and because he could transform himself into a dog, and they had no power over animals. Several times in the novel Harry sees a black dog in the distance, and fears it is a Grim, or terrible omen. But it is only Sirius, watching over his old friend James' son while he searches for Pettigrew. And Pettigrew, in his rat form, has been hiding out as Ron Weasley's pet rodent.

Harry and his friends are in the Shrieking Shack, "the most haunted house in Britain," when they learn all of this. With Pettigrew in hand, they are heading back to Hogwarts when the clouds part, the moon appears, and Professor Lupin is suddenly changed into a werewolf. This produces a lot of confusion, and in the midst of it Pettigrew manages to slip away. Sirius is captured again by the dementors and placed in the tower. Harry and Hermione rescue him with the aid of a hippogriff named Buckbeak, who was reared by Hagrid and is himself under threat of execution. Sirius then flies away on Buckbeak, and the two of them go into hiding. Pettigrew doesn't appear again until we meet him as a servant of Lord Voldemort in *Harry Potter and the Goblet of Fire*.

Discussing the whole business with Dumbledore afterward, Harry expresses his impatience with the reality of things—that Black and Buckbeak, though innocent, are in hiding, and that he himself, at one moment in the Shrieking Shack, stopped Lupin and Black from killing Pettigrew, which means that, in some sense at least, it is *his* fault if Pettigrew somehow helps Voldemort to come back. Dumbledore reminds him of how complicated and diverse the consequences of all our actions are, and says, "This is magic at its deepest, its most impenetrable"[6]—a marvelous statement about the tangled mystery of existence, and a reminder, to us, of Jesus' parable about the wheat and the weeds, and how they must grow together, inseparable until the end of time.

If the existence of hippogriffs and other magical beasts in the Potter narratives bothers Christian minds, it should be recalled that so-called *bestiaries,* or collections of stories about various beasts, both real and mythical, were extremely popular among Christians in the Middle Ages. The earliest of these books that we know is the fourth-century *Physiologus,* variously attributed to an unknown scholar of that name, to St. Jerome, translator of the Vulgate, and to St. Ambrose, bishop of Milan. Drawing on descriptions of strange beasts from Hebrew, Indian, and Egyptian lore, as well as the classical reports of such figures as Aristotle and Pliny, it gave very imaginative accounts of the creatures' appearances and used them to frighten people and (hopefully) increase their faith in Christ.

The genre developed rapidly as a form of Christian education and remained popular until the time of the Renaissance and Reformation. The fanciful beasts were widely used in the art and iconography of the period, decorating churches, cathedrals, Books of Hours (prayer books), and even Bibles. Most of the creatures, such as the gryphon (part lion, part eagle), the unicorn (part horse, part goat), the hippocampus (part horse, part dolphin), the yala (part lion, part elephant), the basilisk (part bird, part reptile), the aphisbaena (reptile heads at both ends), the mermaid (part fish, part woman), and the merman (part fish, part man), were imbued with Christian qualities and used to instruct people in Christian virtues. The unicorn was especially sacred as a representation of Christ. According to popular belief, it was attracted by the Virgin Mary; so hunters used portraits of Mary to try to lure it into the open and take it captive. Only the dragon was considered unredeemable by Christian artists, for it was supposedly derived from the devil himself, and from the serpent that enticed Adam and Eve in the Garden of Eden. Therefore it was invariably represented as an enemy of human beings, and was shown either threatening them or being slain by Christ or St. George.

The countless saints' legends that developed as part of Christian lore in the Middle Ages were likewise filled with allusions to strange creatures imported from secular sources. The famous St. Anthony, for example, was said to have been assisted once by a centaur (half man, half horse), and to have been fed by a satyr (half man, half goat).

With her use of centaurs, unicorns, hippogriffs, and other fanciful beasts, J. K. Rowling is only reminding us of our very colorful past, which, like any past, always consciously or unconsciously impinges, often in important ways, on the present and the future. When Lord Voldemort feeds on the unicorn in *Harry Potter and the Sorcerer's Stone,* for example, the gruesome image is tantamount to a recrucifixion of Christ. Voldemort restores himself by drinking the blood of Christ. Evil regains its strength by feeding on all that is good and holy.

ONCE MORE, WITH PASSION

In the fourth novel, *Harry Potter and the Goblet of Fire,* which Rowling has confessed was her most difficult to write and is pivotal to the three remaining narratives, we learn how truly interwoven good and evil are as Lord Voldemort recovers vitality and calls on his hidden disciples to join him in his bid to take over the world. Weakened at the beginning of the novel to the point of possessing no bodily vitality, and completely dependent on the aid of his servant Pettigrew (from the third novel), now always called Wormtail, Voldemort schemes his total revitalization, including having his own body again.

Central to his plan is a fabulous international Triwizard Tournament, planned with great secrecy by the Ministry of Magic, and held at Hogwarts. Each of three great wizard schools, Beauxbatons in France, Durmstrang in Germany, and of course Hogwarts in Britain, will put forth its champions, of which one from each institution will be selected by the Goblet of Fire to represent that school in the actual competition. The judges announce that candidates must be at least seventeen years of age, as the contest will be very dangerous and require advanced competency in wizardry. The goblet selects a famous Quidditch star, Viktor Krum, from Durmstrang; a tall, beautiful girl, Fleur Delacour, from Beauxbatons; and Cedric Diggory, a modest, handsome young Quidditch player, from Hogwarts. Then the goblet confounds even the judges by spitting out the name of a fourth contestant, Harry Potter. No one appears to know how Harry's name even got into the goblet, as he is three years under the age requirement, but the goblet's will is honored and he is accepted as a bona fide contestant.

There are three trials for the participants, spread over the remainder of the school year, and each is a race against time. First, each contestant must successfully remove a golden egg from the nest of a fierce, fire-breathing dragon. Second, each must rescue a person of great meaning to him or her who has been captured and is bound in the land of the merpeople, deep under the school lake. And, third, each must thread his or her way through a large maze filled with hazards (dragons, a troll, Blast-Ended Skrewts, boggarts, and giant spiders) to reach the Triwizard Cup at the center and lay hands on it before the others, thus claiming victory.

Unknown to the judges, however, Voldemort learns about the contest and uses one of his followers, Barty Crouch, son of a prominent wizard minister and one of the competition's judges, to make sure Harry wins. The reason he wants Harry to win is that the Triwizard Cup has been transformed into a magical Portkey, so that the moment Harry touches it, it will instantly transport him to the cemetery where Voldemort's father is buried and many of his servants have gathered. But Harry, trying to help his fellow competitor, Cedric Diggory, allows Cedric to touch it with him, and they are transported together to the cemetery. Surprised to see Cedric there, Voldemort executes him on the spot.

Following a magical rite which requires some of Harry's blood, Voldemort is restored to power, and his followers all give a great cheer. It is now Voldemort's intention to kill Harry and let the world know that he has triumphed over the adversary who nearly destroyed him thirteen years earlier.

But Harry, angered by the death of Cedric as well as those of his parents, resists. He and Voldemort simultaneously exchange curses. Their wands contain feathers from the same phoenix, however, and are so mystically akin that they cancel one another out. A golden filament springs from their tips, encircling the two opponents, so that Voldemort's supporters cannot get close to help him. Then the ghosts of Voldemort's victims materialize out of the end of his wand—including those of Harry's parents. They encourage Harry to hold fast to his wand and continue the duel. He does so, and the force of the contrary curses raises both contestants into the air. Suddenly, Harry is able to break free. He quickly recovers the cup that is a Portkey, and, bearing Cedric's body with him, escapes to Hogwarts.

There, we discover that Professor Mad-Eye Moody, who has been Harry's friend, is not really Moody at all, but young Barty Crouch, who has transformed himself into Moody by taking Polyjuice Potion. The real Moody has been locked up in his own magic trunk. There is a tense confrontation between Albus Dumbledore, who sees the crisis clearly, and Cornelius Fudge, the Minister of Magic who always wants to compromise or "fudge" things, over what must be done to contain Voldemort's power. Dumbledore wants to approach the giants and enlist them in the fight against the Dark Lord, but Fudge, a purist who has never liked dealing with nonwizards of any kind, refuses. So *Harry Potter and the Goblet of Fire* ends with everything resolved except the future, and the stage is clearly set for terrible battles with Voldemort in the next three novels.

Once more Rowling has underlined the real nature of evil in the world. It is never a simple matter, with a satanic power pulling the strings on millions of selfish, churlish minions. Voldemort is indeed satanic, but his power waxes and wanes according to the fidelity of his followers. And the followers themselves are not always faithful. Professor Snape, head of the Slytherin House at Hogwarts, bears Voldemort's Dark Mark on his body, but has successfully resisted the call to return to him. So has Professor Karkaroff, the suspicious-acting head of the Durmstrang delegation, who flees into hiding when he realizes Voldemort is trying to reassemble his forces. And poor Barty Crouch (the elder), a wizard bureaucrat who has developed a reputation for scrupulosity in searching out and punishing Voldemort's followers, the Death Eaters, becomes hopelessly entangled in evil when he saves his son from Azkaban and then realizes his son is instrumental in helping Voldemort return to power.

Even Harry Potter himself is tangentially involved in Voldemort's resurrection, for his blood was an essential ingredient in the formula for the Dark Lord's restoration in the cemetery. Harry knows this. He feels guilty for having suggested that he and Cedric Diggory claim the Triwizard Cup together, thus involving Cedric in the journey with the Portkey and ending in his death. He refuses to keep the thousand-galleon prize money, and gives it to Fred and George Weasley to open a joke shop, which he sees as a small antidote against the gloom produced by evil in the world.

A friend asked me if Harry really grows in the novels. Of course he does. When we meet him in *Harry Potter and the Sorcerer's Stone,* he is a naïve eleven-year-old whose real knowledge of evil is limited to the crass, objectionable qualities of the Dursley household. At the end of *Harry Potter and the Goblet of Fire,* he is a somber, wary young adolescent, cognizant of the innumerable dark strands woven into the pattern of life. "We could all do with a few laughs," he tells Fred and George. "I've got a feeling we're going to need them more than usual before long."[7]

THE GAME
OF LIFE

CHAP. 3.

UIDDITCH IS SURELY one of the most fantastic inventions of J. K. Rowling's always imaginative and innovative fiction. A game easily worthy of witches and wizards, involving lightning speed, dexterity, teamwork, racing brooms, and not one but *four* balls, three of which are aggressively *alive,* it far surpasses football, baseball, basketball, soccer, hockey, horse racing, and car racing, all of whose actions it at least partially imitates, combines, and sublimates. Nor is it extraneous to the fateful struggle between good and evil, for it always stands symbolically at the very center of that struggle, so that it both mimics and actually becomes the struggle. Its very name is brilliant: Quidditch, from the Latin *quid,* meaning "what," and instantly recognizable for its relationship to one of the great terms in Western philosophy since the Middle Ages, and especially since the advent of the modern existentialist movement created by Martin Heidegger and Jean-Paul Sartre. The *-ch* at the end bestows a certain chthonian flavor on the name that is most appropriate for a game played by witches and wizards.

Quiddity or *quidditas,* whose pedigree goes back at least to Duns Scotus, a philosopher from the little town of Duns, not far from Rowling's Edinburgh, is the *this*ness of things, the essential, undismissable reality of them, as opposed to mere dreams, fantasies, and the imagination. It is simply the way things are in their irreducible being, the unadorned, unavoidable haecceity or uniqueness of existence. And Quidditch, with its remarkable imitation of life, in which its fans are caught up in life and its players actually stand at the precise, existential center of the game of life, is the essence of quiddity. When it is happening, as is true to only a slightly lesser degree in most major sporting events today, it is hard to distinguish between it and life itself; in fact, it represents life so quintessentially that it actually becomes *larger than life!* It isn't any wonder that, as Rowling says in *Harry Potter and the Sorcerer's Stone,* "Everyone from wizarding families talked about Quidditch constantly."[1]

There are seven players on each of two teams in a Quidditch match. Three of the seven are called Chasers, and they spend their time chasing a red ball about the size of a soccer ball called the Quaffle and trying to put it through one of six hoops mounted fifty feet in the air. (Harry describes the Chasers' actions as "sort of like basketball on broomsticks with six hoops."[2] One player on each team is a Keeper. It is the Keeper's job to fly around the hoops and prevent the other side from scoring. There are two players on each team called

Beaters. The Beaters serve two functions: They rocket around the playing area trying to knock opposing players off their brooms, and they attempt to deflect the Bludgers, the two lively black balls, slightly smaller than the Quaffle, which zoom about dangerously toward the players during the contest. There is a seventh player on each team called the Seeker. This is a smaller, lighter player who buzzes about, often high above or around the periphery of the other action, looking for the Golden Snitch, the small fourth ball, which has wings and darts about so quickly that it is difficult to see. The game of Quidditch isn't ever over until the Snitch is caught by one of the Seekers, so games have been known to go on for months. Harry Potter shows such amazing talent with a racing broom the first time he rides one that he is instantly marked for a Seeker.

It is highly interesting that Rowling calls this seventh player a Seeker, a word often applied today to persons whose concern for true spirituality leads them from religion to religion and philosophy to philosophy, rarely resting long in any one place but always searching for the essence of a higher humanity. (Such activity is of course considered a no-no by most conservative Christians. Richard Abanes, in *Harry Potter and the Bible,* for example, pillories "the current atmosphere of 'spirituality' where occult-related ideas and values not only are accepted, but also often are viewed far more positively than Christian-based beliefs and concepts of morality."[3]

Rowling's use of "Snitch" is also worthy of attention. Although lexicographers are uncertain of its origin, it is probably related to the word *snatch,* from the Middle English *snac-chen,* which meant "to give a sudden snap" to something, or "to seize peremptorily." (The use of *snitch* to designate a tattler or betrayer probably derives from the idea that this person "snaps up" the perpetrator of a crime or misdemeanor.) The Snitch, whose sudden capture by a Seeker ends a game, may be symbolic, in its goldenness, uncanny speed, and almost total elusiveness, of the essence of life itself. Life at its best is hard to capture and pin down. Only the most talented persons—or the luckiest—manage to catch it during their days on earth. Harry Potter, as one of the most talented Seekers in the history of Hogwarts—in one game he sets a new record by catching the Snitch in only five minutes—is a rare personality, embodying the finest traditions of the search for a golden existence.

The question of how one finds and seizes the good life has occupied human philosophies from time immemorial. It is central to all the great religions of the world. And in the Harry Potter tales, the answer to the question is identical to the answer given by the Judeo-Christian tradition: It consists of obedience to God and faithful service to the community. "[God] has told you, O mortal, what is good," says the Hebrew prophet Micah, "and what does the Lord require of you but to do justice, and to love kindness, and to walk humbly with your God?"[4]

Contrary to conservative Christian complaints, the entire system of ethics in the Potter stories—Richard Abanes refers to it contemptuously as "Potterethics"—is perfectly congruent with the ethics of Jesus in the Gospels. It pits goodness and mercy, as exemplified in the behavior of Harry, Ron, Hermione, Hagrid, Dumbledore, and the good wizards, against greed, selfishness, and contempt in the Dursleys, Voldemort, Quirrell, Malfoy, Crouch, and all the bad wizards of the various novels.

Consider the character of the headmaster. Dumbledore, whose last name may seem puzzling because it means "bumblebee," as I pointed out earlier, has a giveaway first name. Albus is surely related to Albion, the poetic name for England, which was in turn derived from the name of one of Poseidon's sons in Greek mythology. But it is even more obviously borrowed from the Latin *alb* and the French *albus,* which mean "white" and provide the name "alb" for the tunic or vestment worn by a priest. Also, in the early church, albs were worn by baptismal candidates from the Saturday before Easter until the Sunday after Easter, which is sometimes called Alb Sunday. A saintly man who is both wise and compassionate, Dumbledore could hardly be more selfless and godly.

On the other hand, Draco Malfoy, who is Harry's nemesis at the school and in the Quidditch matches, has a first name that in Latin means "dragon" or "serpent." His last name aptly means "bad faith," from the French *mal foi*—a term used even by the atheistic Jean-Paul Sartre to describe the behavior of those who exist without authenticity and spiritual awareness. Malfoy is snide, conniving, and totally untrustworthy. Even the youngest children reading about him in the novels or seeing him on film take an instant dislike to him, for they recognize him as a contemptible, despicable human being. And when we meet his father, Lucius, in *Harry Potter and the Chamber of Secrets* and subsequent novels, we realize that the apple hasn't fallen far from the tree—he is perhaps even more unbearable than his son.

There are clearly two ways in Rowling's novels, one good and the other bad. One leads to life and the other leads to death. The contrast could not be more vividly delineated.

THE MODEST HERO

One reason Harry is so endearing to the hordes of children who love him is his invincible modesty and humility. He can never get used to the way he is instantly recognized by other wizards and fêted for his survival of Voldemort's attack on him when he was an infant. Typical is the description of the way he is received by Gilderoy Lockhart, in *Harry Potter and the Chamber of Secrets,* when he and the Weasley family go to buy their schoolbooks at Flourish and Blotts. Lockhart recognizes him immediately, and, being an inveterate self-publicist, maneuvers Harry into a photo with him and uses Harry to curry favor with the crowd in the store.

Lockhart, whose first name means "gold king" or "gilded king," is the very picture of a blowhard, one who constantly puffs himself up. As the new Professor of Defense Against the Dark Arts at Hogwarts, he never misses a chance to toot his own horn or shower himself with confetti. An author who has traveled the world appropriating the stories of real heroes who defeated werewolves and various curses, then performing a Memory Charm on them so that they didn't remember that the stories were theirs, he has concocted a brilliant false pedigree for himself to go with his wavy hair and thousand-watt smile. In the end, he proves to be a coward and an impostor, and, when one of his own Memory Charms backfires on him, can't even remember who he was.

Harry, by contrast, is a shrinking violet, and prefers never to be in the limelight. When he first meets Ron Weasley, who becomes his closest friend at Hogwarts, Ron is frightened and impressed by Harry's saying Voldemort's name aloud. When he tries to say something about it, Harry remonstrates: "I'm not trying to be *brave* or anything, saying the name, I just never knew you shouldn't. See what I mean? I've got loads to learn. . . . I bet," he adds, voicing for the first time something that has been worrying him a lot lately, "I bet I'm the worst in the class."[5] When the gibbering house-elf Dobby visits Harry at the Dursleys' and fawns over him because of his greatness and goodness, Harry becomes red in the face and protests, "Whatever you've heard about my greatness is a load of rubbish. I'm not even top of my year at Hogwarts."[6]

"Harry Potter is humble and modest," says Dobby in reverence. "Harry Potter speaks not of his triumph over He-Who-Must-Not-Be-Named."[7]

And when the obsequious, adoring, first-year student Colin Creevey follows Harry everywhere, taking snapshots of him, Harry cringes and attempts to dodge out of sight. At a

Quidditch training session, the arena is filled with the sound of clicking, coming from somewhere in the stands. The coach and players look up and see Colin shooting away.

"Look this way, Harry!" he calls. "This way!"

"Who's that?" asks Fred Weasley.

"No idea," Harry lies, putting on a burst of speed that carries him "as far away as possible from Colin."[8]

Walking humbly with one's God, as the prophet Micah recommended, is a sign of inner goodness. Harry's head is not turned by recognition and popularity because he knows these do not in themselves constitute worthiness. His own worth—for he is not, once he gets away from the Dursley household, a particularly self-doubting boy—stems from a sense of being in tune with goodness, not from possessing or exemplifying it.

The same could obviously be said of Jesus, who chided one admirer, "Why do you call me good? There is only one who is good, and that is God,"[9] and who on at least one occasion when a crowd was so excited about him that they wanted to make him a king, slipped away and returned temporarily to obscurity.[10] The Fourth Gospel operates from an extremely high Christology, of course, depicting Jesus as the cocreator of the world who came among human beings with omniscience, self-awareness, and the clearly defined purpose of becoming the Savior of the world; but in the Synoptic Gospels, written several years before this more sublime interpretation emerged, Jesus is the humble Galilean chosen by God for a mission that carries him into conflict with the political and ideological powers of the day, and he never loses the rough, country simplicity of a man who is in love with God, not with himself.

A COMMITMENT TO RIGHT

Another thing children have said they like about Harry Potter is that he lies or fudges the truth when he has to, but only in the service of a right action or a good purpose. Professor Snape constantly accuses him of bending or violating the Hogwarts rules to suit himself, and this he certainly does. When he is forbidden to go to Hogsmeade, the wizarding village that upper students love to visit on special days, because he did not secure Uncle Vernon's permission, he dons the Invisibility Cloak he inherited from his father and goes anyway. And he often uses the cloak to get him and his friends Ron and Hermione around the halls of Hogwarts or down to Hagrid's cottage by the woods after hours, when they are sleuthing for clues or simply want to visit Hagrid. He comes into possession of the magical Marauder's Map, developed by his father and a little band of friends, which not only shows all the hidden passages of the Hogwarts castle and its environs but reveals, at any given moment, where everybody in the castle is. Such instruments are strictly forbidden. But Harry delights in the map and uses it frequently—though only in the service of good.

It is this kind of disregard for the rules and regulations that is assailed so vigorously by Richard Abanes in *Harry Potter and the Bible*. Assiduously chronicling the lies told by Harry and his friends, and the number of times they fracture regulations, Abanes accuses Rowling of extolling "deceitful behavior" as "a valuable tool for successful living," and deplores the model this sets before young readers. He and his conservative friends obviously much prefer the anal behavior of Percy Weasley, whom he exalts as a good character for zealously following the rules.

What conservative Christians often forget, however, is that Jesus, the founder of their religion, invariably exhibited a healthy disrespect for rules and regulations, especially when they were followed for their own sake or stood in the way of some worthy goal or achievement. He called the Pharisees "whitewashed sepulchers," who made the outside of their lives appear clean and inviting, while inside they were filled with death and putrefaction. They were always straining at gnats, he said, and swallowing camels. They liked to be seen standing on street corners praising God, when in fact they should be fleeing from the wrath of God. They were always looking for specks in their neighbors' eyes, when they could hardly see for the great planks in their own. It was Jesus' healthy disregard for the rules—healing people on the Sabbath and letting his disciples pluck grain on the Sabbath, among other things—that alienated the Pharisees and led eventually to their insistence that the Romans crucify him. Not once in his ministry, if we disregard Judas' betrayal at the end, did Jesus have problems with the 'am ha'aretz, or ignorant and nonobservant Jews of his time. On the contrary, it was the scrupulously educated and strictly observant Pharisees and Sadducees who dogged him relentlessly and brought about his death.

It is therefore highly ironic—and tragic—that a certain strain of Christianity in our time should loudly proclaim its unyielding loyalty to Christ and his religion while so flagrantly disregarding the actual character of the man himself and the way he consistently opposed a religion of rules and hypocrisy. I cannot help agreeing strongly with Professor Marcus Borg, who says, in *Meeting Jesus Again for the First Time,* that Jesus came not to remind us to be holy as God is holy but to be *compassionate as God is compassionate.*[11]

Despite his propensity for dealing loosely with truth and regulations when it is convenient, Harry is invariably oriented toward the service of goodness and high ideals. His father, who was high-minded and courageous, and his mother, who was loving and protective, have passed on to Harry their best qualities, and those who knew James and Lily Potter when they were students at Hogwarts a generation earlier often express pleasure at the way the son embodies the parents' noblest traits.

Rowling is fully conscious of the way she sets forth Christian ethical priorities in her books. In *Harry Potter and the Chamber of Secrets,* when Harry is debriefing everyone in Professor McGonagall's office about what happened in the chamber between him and Voldemort, McGonagall eagerly prompts him to continue his story by saying, "Very well, so you found out where the entrance was—*breaking a hundred school rules into pieces along the way, I might add* [italics mine]—but how on *earth* did you all get out of there alive, Potter?"[12] Rowling gives children the credit for knowing right from wrong about infractions of rules. She knows they bend and break the rules all the time. What is important is not how punctilious they are in observing rules but what their real character is, and what they do with their lives.

Like the Jesus of the Synoptic Gospels, who "set his face to go to Jerusalem"[13] as the political currents flowed against him and he could almost certainly anticipate imprisonment or death, Harry stubbornly moves on toward any important confrontation, regardless of the pain or danger involved. When he knows Hagrid is suffering in his gamekeeper's cottage, he sneaks out to see him despite the consequences if Harry is caught. When he is warned not to return to Hogwarts because something terrible awaits him if he does, he goes anyway. When Sibyll Trelawney, the professor of Divination, predicts Harry's death on an almost weekly basis, he waves it off with a shake of his head and pursues his path as truly as if she had foretold only success and happiness.

His courage and determination are symbolized by his behavior in a Quidditch match with the Slytherin team after Lucius Malfoy has bought the entire Slytherin team "the fastest racing brooms gold could buy." The match has hardly begun when a heavy black Bludger comes hurtling toward Harry with such speed that he barely avoids it. George Weasley, one of the Gryffindor Beaters, gives the Bludger a powerful whack in the direction of a Slytherin player, but it changes course in midair and shoots straight for Harry again. Harry drops quickly to avoid it, and George hits it again, this time toward Draco Malfoy, the Slytherin Seeker. Again the Bludger acts like a boomerang and heads toward Harry. Harry puts on a burst of speed toward the other end of the pitch. But once more he hears the Bludger "whistling along behind him."

What is happening? Bludgers never behave like this.

Fred Weasley, the other Gryffindor Beater, is waiting at the end of the pitch, and Harry ducks as Fred sends the Bludger away. "Gotcha!" yells Fred. But the Bludger, as though "magnetically attracted to Harry," heads for him again, forcing him to fly away at full speed.

The Gryffindors call time out. Wood, the player-coach, wants to know what's happening. George Weasley says that somebody has tampered with the Bludger. The Slytherins have obviously bewitched it so it won't leave Harry alone.

A few minutes back into the game, just as Harry spots the Snitch, the Bludger hits him at last, smashing his elbow and breaking his arm. The pain is dazzling. Harry slides sideways on his rain-glazed broom, barely managing to hold on. His useless arm dangling by his side, he swerves once more to miss a frontal assault by the Bludger. Then, edging toward the Snitch, he takes his good hand off the broom, gripping the shaft only with his legs, and seizes the prize. Riddled with pain, he lands his broom, says vaguely, "We've won," and faints.[14]

It is the kind of courage that leads people forward despite powerful opposition—even to a cross!

DECENCY AND FAIR PLAY

Part of the age-old formula of the battle between good and evil is that the good always play fairly and honestly, while the bad use any means available to win. As Professor Quirrell sums up the evil viewpoint for Harry in *Harry Potter and the Sorcerer's Stone*, "There is no good and evil, there is only power, and those too weak to seek it."[15] But unlike the followers of Voldemort, Harry is committed to fairness and justice, as are all his friends and most of the students at Hogwarts.

As Madam Hooch, the referee, says to the Gryffindors and Slytherins at the beginning of Harry's very first Quidditch match, "Now, I want a nice fair game, all of you."[16]

But, of all the four Hogwarts houses, Slytherin, whose emblem is the serpent, is most inclined to play unfairly. The game has been under way only a few minutes when Harry spots the Golden Snitch and zooms toward it. He almost has it when *wham!*, a Slytherin player named Marcus Flint rams him, knocking him off course. A still inexperienced player, Harry holds on to his broom for dear life.

"Foul!" cry the Gryffindors.

Someone in the stands, familiar with soccer, cries, "Send him off, ref! Red card!"

Even the game announcer finds it difficult not to take sides. "So—after that obvious and disgusting bit of cheating—," he says. Professor McGonagall growls to him that he is to be impartial. "I mean," he continues, "after that open and revolting foul—"[17] We understand, because our instincts as readers are always with those who play fairly and against those who don't.

Fairness is as natural to Harry as breathing. He never considers taking unwarranted advantage of other players. In the great Triwizard Tournament in *Harry Potter and the Goblet of Fire*, Harry has learned from Hagrid that the first trial of the tournament will involve dealing with enormous dragons. He also knows that both Madam Maxime of Beauxbatons and Professor Karkaroff of Durmstrang are aware of the dragons, and thus infers that their champions will likewise be informed. The one contestant who would not know is Cedric Diggory, the other Hogwarts champion. So Harry contrives to get alone with Cedric and tell him.

"They've got four, one for each of us," he says, "and we've got to get past them."

"Are you sure?" asks Cedric.

"Dead sure," says Harry.

A minute later, Cedric asks, "Why are you telling me?"

"It's just . . . fair, isn't it?" he says. "We all know now . . . we're on an even footing, aren't we?"[18]

Harry's sense of fairness and loyalty extends to almost anybody who deserves it. He cannot stand Draco Malfoy and his bullying friends, who sneer at others, skulk around like young Death Eaters, and can be trusted only to be untrustworthy. But to everyone else—Ron, Hermione, Dumbledore, Hagrid, Mr. and Mrs. Weasley, Mad-Eye Moody, even Hagrid's big hippogriff, Buckbeak—his fealty is never questioned or compromised. His sense of right is as unfailing as the magnetic needle that finds true North.

It isn't something Harry works at. He never sits and thinks, "Now, I must behave this way in order to fulfill my duty to Hogwarts and wizardry in general." It is simply instinctive in him to be honest, fair, and faithful.

The same is true of his close friends. Ron is perhaps more prone than Harry to cut corners. But both he and Hermione have an innate sense of decency and fairness. In Hermione's case, it comes out particularly in *Harry Potter and the Goblet of Fire,* when she takes up the cause of the house-elves who prepare the meals and keep Hogwarts clean. We met the first house-elf, Dobby, in *Harry Potter and the Chamber of Secrets*. Harry was instrumental in setting Dobby free from his indenturedness to Lucius Malfoy. In *Harry Potter and the Goblet of Fire,* we meet Dobby's friend Winky, a female house-elf who belongs to Barty Crouch of the Ministry of Magic. When Crouch fires her for being involved in a fracas at the Quidditch World Cup, she shows up at Hogwarts as part of the house-elf team that does the menial work in the castle.

Hermione is present when Crouch fires Winky and becomes immediately incensed at the wizards' treatment of her.

> "The way they were treating her!" Hermione said furiously. "Mr. Diggory, calling her 'elf' all the time . . . and Mr. Crouch! He knows she didn't do it and he's still going to sack her! He didn't care how frightened she'd been, or how upset she was—it was like she wasn't even human!"[19]

"Elf rights," an issue similar to black rights or women's rights, becomes one of Hermione's themes in the novel, and she sounds off on it at every opportunity. When Ron Weasley says, "We've been working like house-elves here!,"[20] a phrase reminiscent of the derogatory term "house-niggers" common in the U.S. South until the late twentieth century, she becomes upset and reveals to him and Harry a box of badges she has fashioned with the acronym S.P.E.W. on them. The letters stand for the Society for the Promotion of Elfish Welfare, and signal the beginning of Hermione's campaign to free the Hogwarts elves, and pay them for work performed. Echoing the conservative voice in the battle for racial integration, Ron insists to her, "Hermione—open your ears. They. Like. It. They *like* being enslaved!"[21] And it seems to be true. On more than one occasion, Winky cries, throws herself on the floor, and protests that elves *want* to work and aren't interested in being paid for what they do. But Hermione is determined. She will not be happy until the elves' slavery is ended and they begin to receive representation on various wizards' boards and agencies.

All of this is integral to the plot of the novel, as we learn, because Winky's fidelity to the Crouch family has caused her to keep a secret that, had it been revealed, might have saved the wizard community a lot of grief. But the importance of the issue to Hermione is revelatory of the decent inner nature of those who belong to the forces of good in the world. Perhaps it is not to Harry's credit that he isn't as perturbed about the freedom and compensation of the house-elves as Hermione is, although his maneuvering of Lucius Malfoy into giving Dobby his freedom indicates that his heart is in the right place. And Ron, at times, looks positively selfish in his interest in the food provided by the house-elves and in his twitting of Hermione about her campaign.

But their varied levels of concern for the house-elves is a fairly accurate mirror of Christian compassion toward the Negroes during the struggle for integration in America, and probably in South Africa as well. Some Christians campaigned tirelessly for human rights. Others believed the social system was working well as it was and that only the radical young blacks really wanted equality with whites. And some, of course, actually resisted change, believing God had ordained the system as it was.

There is little doubt where Rowling's sympathies lie. With the all-seeing eye of the novelist, she understands the nature of the house-elves and their desire to live in a menial capacity. But she also cares about those who serve—she herself has been a secretary and a secondary-school teacher—and obviously sympathizes with Hermione's passion to bring liberty and equality to those who work so tirelessly behind the scenes at Hogwarts. When Hermione becomes exasperated with Ron and pleads, her eyes flashing, *"House-elves!* Not once, in over a thousand pages, does *Hogwarts, A History* mention that we are all colluding in the oppression of a hundred slaves!,"[22] she is speaking for Rowling and all decent people everywhere who care about the way history and cultures often forget enslaved or abused people.

Whether at Quidditch, in the classroom, in the social structures of Hogwarts, or in the mixed world of Muggles and wizards beyond Hogwarts, the good people in Rowling's narratives never move far from the reminder of Jesus: "In everything do to others as you would have them do to you; for this is the law and the prophets."[23]

A READINESS TO SACRIFICE SELF

"This is my commandment," says Jesus to his disciples at the Last Supper, "that you love one another as I have loved you. No one has greater love than this, to lay down one's life for one's friends."[24]

Self-sacrifice may have occurred in people before the Christian era, but never with the recommendation and frequency it enjoyed after the example of Christ on the cross, who willingly tendered his life "a ransom for many."[25] The theme of giving one's life in behalf of others became common in early Christian culture, and through the intervening centuries the church has continued to honor the love and courage of those who rise to the call for such an action.

Jaroslav Pelikan, Sterling Professor of History at Yale University, says in his widely read *Jesus Through the Centuries— His Place in the History of Culture:*

> The followers of Jesus came very early to the conclusion that he had lived in order to die, that his death was not the interruption of his life at all but its ultimate purpose. Even by the most generous reading, the Gospels give us informa-

tion about less than a hundred days in the life of Jesus; but for the last two or three days of his life, they provide a detailed, almost hour-by-hour scenario. And the climax of that scenario is the account of Good Friday and of his three hours on the cross. The Apostles' Creed and the Nicene Creed recognized this when they moved directly from his birth "from the Virgin Mary" to his crucifixion "under Pontius Pilate." What was said of the thane of Cawdor in *Macbeth* was true preeminently of Jesus: "Nothing in his life/ Became him like the leaving it."[26]

If there is indeed a Christ-likeness in the Harry Potter stories, it must somehow involve the theme of self-sacrifice—of the hero's willingness to brave threat and danger for others, possibly even undergoing self-immolation. Harry is of course a child in the stories—only eleven at the outset and eighteen at the end of them—and it is still anyone's guess whether Rowling will have him die at the conclusion of the final book. But again and again he proves his readiness to risk everything in behalf of others, fulfilling Christ's ideal of laying down his life for his friends.

In *Harry Potter and the Sorcerer's Stone*, Harry and Ron come to the aid of Hermione when she is endangered by a giant, loathsome troll. Professor Dumbledore has warned of the troll's presence and ordered all students to their rooms. Harry and Ron are en route to their dorm when they remember that Hermione wasn't present and didn't know about the troll, so they go to look for her. On their way, they catch sight of the monster. It is twelve feet tall, with "a great lumpy body like a boulder" and "a small bald head perched on top like a coconut." Its short legs are thick as tree trunks, and it carries a huge wooden club, which it drags along on the floor because its arms are so long.

The troll enters the girls bathroom. The boys see that the door key is in the lock. They edge toward the door. Harry leaps forward and turns the key. Happy with their success, the boys turn and run back down the corridor—until they hear a scream from the bathroom and realize Hermione is in there.

Returning to the bathroom is the last thing either wants to do. But they have no choice. Harry opens the door and they run inside. Hermione is against the far wall, looking as if she will faint. The troll is advancing toward her, knocking sinks off as he passes.

"Confuse it!" Harry yells to Ron as he seizes a loose water tap and throws it at the monster. The troll turns, stares at Harry, and starts toward him. Ron throws a metal pipe at it, deflecting its attention. Harry runs around it, grabs Hermione, and tries to propel her toward the door. But she is frozen with terror and cannot move. The troll roars and starts toward Ron.

Harry does something the author calls "both very brave and very stupid." He takes a running jump and manages to fasten his arms around the troll's neck from behind. The troll doesn't notice the frail boy's presence until it suddenly shrieks with pain from the wand Harry has thrust up its nostril. Howling in agony, it now twists and flails its club, trying to throw Harry off or catch him with a blow of the club.

Hermione sinks to the floor in fright, as Ron pulls out his own wand and cries the first spell that comes into his head: *"Wingardium Leviosa!"* The club flies out of the monster's hand, rises in the air, and then descends with enormous force on its head. The troll staggers, then falls flat on its face with a thud that causes the whole room to shudder.

Moments later, three professors arrive. "What on earth were you thinking of?" asks Professor McGonagall. "You're lucky you weren't killed. Why aren't you in your dormitory?"[27] Harry doesn't answer, of course, for they should have been obeying the rules. But in this case a higher rule applied: He and Ron had returned to the bathroom to save Hermione. And they were all disregarding the rules for a simple reason: They were trying to prevent Voldemort from getting control of the Sorcerer's Stone.

Later in the same story, when Harry, Ron, and Hermione think Professor Snape is in league with Voldemort and is trying to secure the Sorcerer's Stone for him, Harry says he is going to get to the Stone first—which means disobeying Professor McGonagall's orders not to enter the dungeons where the Stone is, getting past the three-headed dog guarding it, making his way through the Devil's Snare plant that stands in the way, and finding the magic key that will open the final chamber.

Ron says he is mad. Hermione says he can't—he'll be expelled for doing it!

"SO WHAT?" Harry shouted. "Don't you understand? If Snape gets hold of the Stone, Voldemort's coming back!

Haven't you heard what it was like when he was trying to take over? There won't be any Hogwarts to get expelled from! He'll flatten it, or turn it into a school for the Dark Arts! Losing points doesn't matter any more, can't you see? D'you think he'll leave you and your families alone if Gryffindor wins the house cup? If I get caught before I can get to the Stone, well, I'll have to go back to the Dursleys and wait for Voldemort to find me there, it's only dying a bit later than I would have, because I'm never going over to the Dark Side! I'm going through that trapdoor tonight and nothing you two say is going to stop me! Voldemort killed my parents, remember?"[28]

As Christ's sacrifice was infectious among his followers, several of whom were supposedly slain for their faith, Harry's bravery rubs off on Ron and Hermione, who finally accompany him on the quest for the Stone. When Harry's ability as a Seeker has enabled him to spot the right key flying around the room among hundreds of others, and they have entered another chamber on their way, they see that they have to get past an astonishing, lifelike chess set, whose players are taller than they are and come to life as they accept the challenge of crossing the board. Ron, who has been more attentive to chess than Harry, takes the lead. Walking up to a black knight, he reaches out and touches the horse. The horse begins to paw the ground and the knight turns his head toward Ron. Ron tells Harry to take the place of a bishop and Hermione the place of a rook, and he himself leaps astride the horse, as the former pieces move off the board, relinquishing their roles.

The game begins, with Ron directing their moves. "Harry— move diagonally four squares to the right." He does, and the other knight is taken. The white queen smashes him to the floor and drags him off the board, where he lies quite lifeless. The slaughter continues. Every time the white pieces have the opportunity, they ruthlessly take their opponents. A pile of black players lies slumped beside the board. Ron ponders what to do next.

"Yes," he says softly, "it's the only way . . . I've got to be taken." "NO!" shout Harry and Hermione.

"That's chess!" says Ron. "You've got to make some sacrifices! I take one step forward and she'll take me—that leaves you free to checkmate the king, Harry!"[29]

Ron steps forward and the white queen pounces on him. She strikes him across the head so hard with her stone arm that he crashes to the floor. But Harry makes his move and the white king takes off his crown and throws it at Harry's feet. The chessmen part and bow, clearing their way to the door.

Harry himself will of course face Professor Quirrell and Voldemort when he and Hermione get to the Stone. We have already discussed that encounter. But it is heartening to see what a powerful influence for courage and sacrifice Harry has exerted on his friends and disciples.

In *Harry Potter and the Chamber of Secrets,* the house-elf Dobby tries to warn Harry away from Hogwarts because of "terrible things" he knows are going to happen there. Dobby's

master was Lucius Malfoy, who is one of Voldemort's faithful
followers, and Dobby is torn between his earlier fealty to Malfoy and his affection for Harry. His feelings for Harry win out
because Harry's earlier victory over Voldemort gave hope to all
good elves and wizards that the Dark Lord's power was broken. But Dobby knows that awful things are being planned
against the Mudbloods, or Muggle-born wizards, and wants
Harry to leave.

Harry protests that he is not Muggle-born and therefore
has nothing to fear. When Dobby insists that he leave, Harry
says one of his best friends, Hermione, is Muggle-born, and he
will not leave her.

"Harry Potter risks his own life for his friends!" moans
Dobby. "So noble! So valiant! But he must save himself, Harry
Potter must not—"[30]

Harry of course ignores the warning and does indeed risk his
life for his friend—the very action recommended by Jesus at the
Last Supper. And not only that, he soon afterward risks his life
for another student. Draco Malfoy has conjured up a huge black
snake during a demonstration by Professors Lockhart and Snape
at the Dueling Club. When Lockhart makes a clumsy attempt at
making the snake disappear, it flies into the air and falls back to
the floor at the feet of a student named Justin Finch-Fletchley.
Enraged, the serpent raises itself, fangs exposed, to strike.

Without pausing even to think, and completely unaware of
the danger to himself, Harry instinctively rushes forward and
shouts at the snake, "Leave him alone!"[31] This is the episode in
which we learn that Harry speaks Parseltongue, the language

of snakes, which explains his understanding the ominous voice breathing death through the hallways of Hogwarts and his ability, at the climax of the story, to address the monstrous basilisk in the secret chamber. This snake is easily dispatched by Harry's command. But not so, unfortunately, the terrible basilisk under Voldemort's control.

I have already referred to Harry's eager descent into the pipes leading to the secret chamber to rescue Ginny Weasley in terms of Jesus' *descensus ad inferos,* or Descent into Hell. The Descent into Hell, which was mentioned in a sixth-century Gallican creed that expressed the ideas later embodied in the widely used Apostles' Creed of about 750 C.E., pictures Jesus descending into Hades during the three days (or parts of three days) between his death on the cross and his resurrection. In the Middle Ages, it was known as the Harrowing of Hell. Christ supposedly assaulted the gates of hell to free the souls consigned to Satan's power. There were many popular woodcuts of the imaginary event, and, later, many stained-glass windows depicting it.

"I'm going down there," declares Harry when he and Ron behold the bathroom pipe twisting and becoming enlarged, revealing a tubular entrance to the secret chamber below.

"He couldn't not go, not now they had found the entrance to the Chamber, not if there was even the faintest, slimmest, wildest chance that Ginny might be alive."[32]

The way down is "like rushing down an endless, slimy, dark slide." Harry sees more pipes branching off in all directions, and knows he is "falling deeper below the school than even the dungeons." At the bottom is a "dark stone tunnel large enough to stand in"—and it is there, in the inner bowels of the secret chamber, that Harry confronts the hideous basilisk and his old nemesis, Lord Voldemort. Once more, he has risked his life for another without thinking of the danger to himself.

In *Harry Potter and the Goblet of Fire,* Harry not only risks his life to rescue his friend Ron from the merpeople deep under the school lake, but shows his complete disregard for himself when others are at risk of any kind. For the second task of the Triwizard Tournament, the champions' friends have been captured and are being held under a spell by the merpeople. Each champion must elude the giant squid in the lake, a troll, the boggarts, and the horned water demons, or grindylows, and rescue his or her friend from the underwater captivity. But when Harry reaches Ron, he finds not only Ron but Hermione, Cho Chang, and a small girl he recognizes as Fleur Delacour's baby sister. Having used a jagged rock from the bottom of the lake to cut Ron's bindings, he begins to hack at Hermione's too, afraid the other champions will not reach them.

The mermen grab him. "You take your own hostage," says one of them. "Leave the others . . ."

"No way!" says Harry furiously.[33]

Cedric Diggory, the other Hogwarts champion, shows up and cuts Cho loose. He tells Harry that Krum and Delacour are on their way for the others. Krum arrives and helps to free Hermione. But Delacour still has not come. Harry attempts to free her sister but is threatened by the mermen. He pulls out his wand, warns them to fall back, and finishes freeing her.

Holding her around the waist and grabbing the neck of Ron's robes, he kicks off from the bottom. It is difficult going, bearing two captives instead of one, but he eventually makes it back to safety. Fleur Delacour, he learns, was attacked by grindylows and could not make it to rescue her sister.

Professor Dumbledore, sizing up the situation, crouches at the edge of the lake and has a conversation with the chief of the merpersons. He reveals to the other judges what transpired beneath the water, and they award Harry forty-five points out of a possible fifty, for displaying "moral fiber," even though he returned last from the mission. The amount puts him in first place with Cedric Diggory. But Harry has shown no concern for his standing in the contest—it was the lives of the captives that really mattered to him.

LOVING OTHERS

"No one has greater love than this," said Jesus, "to lay down one's life for one's friends."[34] Love and sacrifice are intimately connected, and the bottom line of the whole Christian message is love. God sent his Son into the world, says the Gospel of John, because God loved the world.[35] And the writer of the Epistle of 1 John says:

> Beloved, let us love one another, because love is from God; everyone who loves is born of God and knows God. Whoever does not love does not know God, for God is love.

God's love was revealed among us in this way: God sent his only Son into the world so that we might live through him. In this is love, not that we loved God but that he loved us and sent his Son to be the atoning sacrifice for our sins. Beloved, since God loved us so much, we also ought to love one another. No one has ever seen God; if we love one another, God lives in us, and his love is perfected in us.[36]

When Harry asks Dumbledore, at the end of *Harry Potter and the Sorcerer's Stone,* why Professor Quirrell could not bear to touch him when Voldemort was demanding that Quirrell kill him, Dumbledore says:

"Your mother died to save you. If there is one thing Voldemort cannot understand, it is love. He didn't realize that love as powerful as your mother's for you leaves its own mark. Not a scar, no visible sign . . . to have been loved so deeply, even though the person who loved us is gone, will give us some protection forever. It is in your very skin. Quirrell, full of hatred, greed, and ambition, sharing his soul with Voldemort, could not touch you for this reason. It was agony to touch a person marked by something so good."[37]

In the Christian tradition, all of those who belong to God, and live in God, are transformed by love into a vast commonwealth of souls, a heavenly kingdom, in which love continues to grow stronger and stronger. Because they have been touched by this love, Christians still alive pray for the dead, and it is believed that the dead pray for them as well. Charles Williams' novels *All Hallows' Eve, War in Heaven,* and *Descent into Hell* are about this invisible but extremely powerful community of love.

In the dramatic scene in *Harry Potter and the Goblet of Fire* where Harry's and Voldemort's wands clash, producing an amazing gold filament between them, the ghosts of Voldemort's victims begin issuing from the end of his wand—first Cedric Diggory, whom he has just slain, then Frank Bryce and Bertha Jorkins, and finally Harry's parents, James and Lily Potter—and each in turn has words of encouragement for Harry.

"Hold on, Harry," says Cedric's shade.

"You fight him, boy," says Bryce's ghost.

"Don't let go, now!" cries the ghost of Bertha Jorkins. "Don't let him get you, Harry—don't let go!"

"Your mother's coming . . ." says James Potter quietly. "She wants to see you . . . it will be all right . . . hold on. . . ."

"When the connection is broken," says Lily Potter—the golden filament temporarily binding the two wands— "we will linger for only moments . . . but we will give you time . . . you must get to the Portkey, it will return you to Hogwarts . . . do you understand, Harry?"

"Do it now," whispers his father's voice, "be ready to run . . . do it now. . . ."[38]

And Harry runs, dragging Cedric's body with him, dodging behind tombstones, using his wand and a spell to bring the Triwizard Cup within his grasp, and suddenly being whisked away by the Portkey, Cedric's body in tow, back to Hogwarts and safety. It is one of the most dramatic scenes in all the Potter stories, and one of the most revelatory of the spiritual structure behind them. Harry has been saved by what Christians call "the communion of the saints," the fellowship of love that grows out of the divine love and binds all believers' hearts together in holy unity!

At the somber end-of-term dinner in the Great Hall of Hogwarts, Dumbledore tells the assembled faculty and students about Cedric's death and Harry's heroism in resisting Voldemort and returning with Cedric's body. "He risked his own life to return Cedric's body to Hogwarts," says Dumbledore. "He showed, in every respect, the sort of bravery that few wizards have ever shown in facing Lord Voldemort, and for this, I honor him."[39]

Dumbledore turns to Harry and raises his goblet to him. Nearly everyone in the hall follows suit. They murmur Harry's name and drink to him. (Given the eschatological tone of all that has happened, can this be reminiscent of the way Christians lift their cups to Christ in the sacrament of the Lord's Table?) Dumbledore continues, saying that the Triwizard Tournament was organized with the intention of promoting closer ties among wizards all over the world—ties that now "are more important than ever before."

"Every guest in this Hall," he says, "will be welcomed back here at any time, should they wish to come. I say to you all, once again—in the light of Lord Voldemort's return, we are only as strong as we are united, as weak as we are divided. Lord Voldemort's gift for spreading discord and enmity is very great. We can fight it only by showing an equally strong bond of friendship and trust. Differences of habit and language are nothing at all if our aims are identical and our hearts are open."[40]

The Lord of Darkness spreads discord and enmity. The Lord of Light brings love and unity. And, in the final analysis, cleaving to the Light, to love, to unity, is the essence of the good life. Humility, decency, fair play, doing to others as one would have them do to you, being ready to sacrifice self for others, are all part of it. But it is the love of God and the unity of the spirit that raise them all beyond mere individual acts and impart to them a sense of transcendent meaning, that convert them into what the Apostle Paul in the Letter to the Galatians called "the fruit of the Spirit."

And what is the fruit of the Spirit? It is the opposite of what Paul denominated "the works of the flesh":

> Now the works of the flesh are obvious: fornication, impurity, licentiousness, idolatry, sorcery, enmities, strife, jealousy, anger, quarrels, dissensions, factions, envy, drunkenness, carousing, and things like these. I am warning you, as I warned you before: those who do such things will not inherit the kingdom of God.
>
> By contrast, the fruit of the Spirit is love, joy, peace, patience, kindness, generosity, faithfulness, gentleness, and self-control.[41]

Love—above everything!

A MATTER OF CHOICE

One thing Rowling makes abundantly clear, time and again, is that people are the product of the choices they make. To be sure, there seems to be innate goodness or badness in people—it would be hard to imagine Dudley Dursley or Draco Malfoy ever being very reflective about his life and thus doing anything to improve it. But the Harrys, Hermiones, and Rons are constantly weighing the consequences of their actions, *deciding* how they will behave, and contemplating what the results of their decisions may be.

Rowling doesn't preach to her characters. She tends instead to reflect on their nature at the ends of the novels. At the conclusion of *Harry Potter and the Chamber of Secrets,* for example, Harry and Dumbledore are discussing what happened to Harry when he was attacked by the basilisk and Voldemort in the chamber. Harry recalls that Tom Riddle, who is Voldemort's alter ego, said that the two of them were alike. Harry is obviously troubled by this, because even though he is a Gryffindor and Riddle was a Slytherin, the Sorting Hat almost put him in the Slytherin House. And, like Riddle, he speaks Parseltongue, or serpent language.

Dumbledore suggests that Voldemort may have put a little of himself in Harry the night he tried to kill him as a baby—that some of Voldemort's powers were unintentionally transferred to Harry when he received his scar. Harry is thunderstruck by this. "So I *should* be in Slytherin," says

Harry. "The Sorting Hat could see Slytherin's power in me, and it—"

"Put you in Gryffindor," says Dumbledore. "Listen to me, Harry. You happen to have many qualities Salazar Slytherin prized in his hand-picked students. His own very rare gift, Parseltongue—resourcefulness—determination—a certain disregard for rules . . . Yet the Sorting Hat placed you in Gryffindor. You know why that was. Think."

"It only put me in Gryffindor," says Harry in a defeated voice, "because I asked not to go in Slytherin. . . ."

"*Exactly,*" says Dumbledore, beaming. "Which makes you *very different* from Tom Riddle. It is our choices, Harry, that show what we truly are, far more than our abilities."[42]

Our choices, far more than our abilities. This has always been an important theme in the Judeo-Christian faith. "I call heaven and earth to witness against you today," said God to the Israelites, "that I have set before you life and death, blessings and curses. Choose life so that you and your descendants may live, loving the Lord your God, obeying him, and holding fast to him."[43]

"Simon, son of John," said the resurrected Christ to his disciple Simon Peter, "do you love me more than these?" "Yes, Lord," said Peter; "you know that I love you." Jesus said to him, "Feed my lambs."[44] Throughout the history of the Christian church, there has been an emphasis on the believer's choice as the all-important factor in his or her conversion and transformation as a person. Billy Graham's radio and TV programs, the most widely heard and watched evangelical services in the history of the world, were known as *The Hour of Decision*. God is also a chooser, selecting special persons for various tasks that need doing. But the character of those who adhere to the faith is finally determined by the decisions they themselves must make in the course of a lifetime.

Goethe's *Faust* is one of the flowerings of this tradition, and it is Faust's tragedy that he accepts the blandishments of Mephistopheles, thus indenturing himself to the evil one instead of making the harder choice he might have made.

Some have argued that "what will be will be," and that people are predestined or foreordained to become what they do eventually become. Many believe that race or class or family or DNA or some other given is the strongest determining factor in a person's character or behavior. This is the position of Cornelius Fudge, the Minister of Magic, in *Harry Potter and the Goblet of Fire*, when Dumbledore insists, after Voldemort's revitalization, that the ministry must send envoys to the giants and enlist their support in the future contest with darkness. Fudge knows that most wizards are suspicious of the giants and that they would strongly object to his approaching them. It might even mean the end of his career as minister.

"You are blinded," Dumbledore accuses, "by the love of the office you hold, Cornelius! You place too much importance, and you always have done, on the so-called purity of blood! You fail to recognize that it matters not what someone is born, but what they grow to be! Your dementor has just destroyed the last remaining member of a pure-blood family as old as any [Barty Crouch]—and see what that man chose to make of his life! I tell you now—take the steps I have suggested, and you will be remembered, in office or out, as one of the bravest and greatest Ministers of Magic we have ever known. Fail to act—and history will remember you as the man who stepped aside and allowed Voldemort a second chance to destroy the world we have tried to rebuild!"[45]

Rowling is acutely aware of the importance of choices in her own life. She speaks of studying French and Classics instead of English Literature as a mistake she made because her parents said that languages would make her more employable, and of going to London to take a bilingual secretarial course as "an even bigger mistake" because she was totally unsuited to secretarial work.[46] She has also said that she considers her first marriage, to a Portuguese journalist named Jorge Arantes, a mistake.[47]

She says that the writer who has had the most influence on her is Jessica Mitford, who instantly became her hero when she read *Hons and Rebels* at the age of fourteen. She admired Mitford for running away from home to fight in the civil war in Spain, and for charging her father's account for a camera she took with her to record events in that important struggle. "I wished I'd had the nerve to do something like that," says Rowling. "She had tremendous moral courage and did some physically brave things as a human rights activist. . . . She stood up against her family—they were very rich indeed and didn't believe in educating girls—and showed her passion by acting on what she believed, not preaching."[48] Rowling even named her daughter Jessica after Mitford.

But Rowling did make some hard and courageous choices that turned out right for her. One was to continue writing after she had written two unpublished novels and a number of stories. Another was to move to Edinburgh and continue to work on her first Harry Potter story while she strove to meet the qualifications for a postgraduate certificate in education. And yet another was to risk everything on the success of her work and not "waste" her time trying to earn a living while she was writing the second Harry Potter novel. She is clearly a determined woman, and has confirmed in her life story the truth she reiterates constantly in the novels—that people *choose* who they will be, they do not have to accept the characterizations thrust on them by background and happenstance.

Rowling obviously loves certain characters in her stories— wise old Professor Dumbledore, steady Professor McGonagall, huggable Hagrid, the gentle giant, faithful Ron (who is modeled on her friend Sean Harris, the one with the turquoise Ford Anglia), sometimes prickly, sometimes tender, always disciplined and determined Hermione (a lot like herself as a girl, she has confessed), and of course good, stubborn, nerdish Harry Potter. But it is also clear that she deeply admires some other characters, such as Professor Lupin, who has struggled against his history as a werewolf; Sirius Black, who withstood twelve years among the dementors at Azkaban (Rowling has said that the dementors are related to depression and that she has fought against them in her own life)[49]; and even—or especially—the unlikable Professor Severus Snape, who at one time allowed himself to receive the mark of Voldemort but decided to oppose him and continues valiantly to resist the latter's claim on his life.

The good life, however obvious it may appear to the casual observer or the reader of a novel, is not as easy to achieve and maintain as we might think. Often, it must be won again and again through the hard decisions we make about who we will follow and what we wish to become. It is never an assumable possession. Even the Apostle Paul, a stalwart convert to the Christian way of life if there ever was one, confessed that he frequently did the evil he did not want to do instead of the good he wanted to do,[50] and said that in spite of all his successes in following the way of Christ he still had not attained the goal and must continue to press toward it.[51]

It is part of what we like and admire about Harry Potter and the other good characters in J. K. Rowling's stories that, over and over, they are offered choices for their lives and decide to take the high road. Sometimes Harry and his friends compromise their principles on small matters and ignore the rules set down by their superiors. But they are never in error about the things that matter most. When the chips are down, and character lies in the balance, they always make the right decisions, even if those decisions will be punishing to them.

They usually are.

THE MAGICAL,
MYSTICAL WORLD

CHAP. 4.

ONSERVATIVE CHRISTIANS frequently object to the world of wizardry in the Potter novels—all the tricks, potions, spells, and enchanted objects. And, to be sure, there are plenty of these. They abound in the stories, tumbling over one another like jelly beans cascading out of a dime-store dispenser.

There are strange, magical objects, such as the Sorting Hat that places Hogwarts students in their respective houses, the Mirror of Erised ("desire" spelled backward), in which viewers see what they wish to see, a Sneakoscope that lights up when untrustworthy people are around, and a *Monster Book of Monsters,* that snaps at whoever tries to open it. There are fantastic and wonderful candies, such as exploding bonbons, levitating sherbet balls, and bubble gum that fills the air with bubbles that won't pop for days.

There is the famous platform nine and three-quarters at King's Cross Station, used only by the wizards as they are taking the special train to or from Hogwarts, and requiring them to walk directly into the wall between platforms nine and ten—but which Dobby the house-elf closes against Harry and Ron in *Harry Potter and the Chamber of Secrets*. And the glorious Great Hall at Hogwarts, peopled by ghosts as well as wizards, with a ceiling bewitched to look exactly like the sky outside, and twelve great trees at Christmas decorated with hundreds of candles and real hanging icicles. (In Harry's fourth year, the decorations are the most fabulous he has yet seen: everlasting icicles hanging from the marble banisters, the twelve trees adorned by "everything from luminous holly berries to real, hooting, golden owls," and all the usual suits of armor bewitched to sing carols when anybody passes them.) And the wonderful living statues and portraits everywhere, that move and sing and speak and cry, such as the painting described in *Harry Potter and the Prisoner of Azkaban,* in which a short, squat knight in a suit of armor looks out, sees Harry, Ron, and Hermione, and brandishes his sword at them, saying, "Draw, you knaves, you dogs!"[1] But the sword is too long for him, so that when he swings it, it topples him over into the grass.

Nor must we fail to mention the Forbidden Forest, full of deadly, entangling plants, centaurs, unicorns, and gigantic spiders, at whose edge stands the gamekeeper's cottage and the great Whomping Willow, which severely thrashes anybody or anything that comes within reach of its powerful branches. And there is the famous Polyjuice Potion, which allows people to change themselves into other people's forms, and gillyweed, which Harry eats to grow gills and fins when he must rescue

Ron from the merpeople under the lake, and bubotuber pus, a yellowish green liquid that covers Hermione's hands with painful sores, so that she looks "as though she were wearing a pair of thick, knobbly gloves," and dozens of other magical potions and substances. And Wizard Chess, which we have already mentioned, in which the larger-than-life-size chess pieces come alive and play the game violently. And a golden egg that sings underwater. And Mad-Eye Moody's magical eye that rotates constantly, surveying everything in a room. And wands. . . .

Much of the magic performed by wizards is done with the aid of a wand—and not just any wand, but a wand especially suited to its bearer. One of the most charming scenes in all the Potter novels is the one when Harry is first taken by Hagrid to Diagon Alley, the wizards' shopping center in London, and they enter the narrow little shop with the peeling gold letters on the door that read "Ollivanders: Makers of Fine Wands since 382 B.C." Old Mr. Ollivander himself, a small man with silvery, creepy eyes, appears. He recalls exactly every wand he has ever sold, including the one that belonged to James Potter, Harry's father, and, he is sorry to say, the one taken by Lord Voldemort, which was used to kill Harry's parents and then turned on Harry himself.

Measuring Harry very carefully, Mr. Ollivander ("old wander") tells him that every wand contains a magical core— either a unicorn hair, a phoenix tail feather, or the heartstring of a dragon—and that no two wands are exactly alike. After trying several wands, they arrive at precisely the right one for

Harry. Ollivander is struck by the fact that the phoenix that provided a feather for it is the same one that gave a feather for the wand that dealt Harry his scar. Later, of course, we learn that the donor was Fawkes, Dumbledore's pet phoenix that saves Harry's life in the *Chamber of Secrets*. And it is the kinship of the two wands that causes them to react strangely when Harry and Voldemort attempt to use them simultaneously on each other in the cemetery scene in *Harry Potter and the Goblet of Fire*.

(Perhaps it isn't important, but Voldemort's wand is made of oak, while Harry's is fashioned of holly, a wood often associated with Christ, and even, according to one legend, called "Christ's thorn" because it sprang from Christ's footsteps on earth, and its thorny leaves and berries like drops of blood were believed to be symbolic of his suffering.)

The wands are of course used to cast spells of various kinds, and Harry Potter's education at Hogwarts is an induction into a world of spells and curses that is amazing and often bewildering to him. There isn't any room for disbelief in such a world—one simply learns how to control the magical powers that reside in the wand and the nature of things in general. It is interesting that in all of Western legends and fairy tales since Christ, the usual language for spells has been Latin, the language of the Mass and until recent times the official language of Roman Catholicism. There is good reason for this. Clerics in the Middle Ages learned to read Latin in order to perform the sacraments of the church, but ordinary people did not. Hence Latin came to be the language of mystification, and, in the eyes of those who were more cynical, of mumbo jumbo. Even Martin Luther attacked the Mass as a "dumb show" because it was conducted in Latin, and insisted, as a principle of reformation, that both the Bible and the Mass should in the future be translated into the vernacular so that even the plowman in the fields could understand them!

Among the spells we encounter in the Potter stories are *Accio*, the summoning charm (Harry uses it to summon the Triwizard Cup and escape from Voldemort in *Harry Potter and the Goblet of Fire*); *Aparecium*, from the root word *appareo*, which causes invisible messages to appear; *Deletrius*, from the Latin *deleo*, which deletes or causes things to disappear; *Obliviate*, from "oblivion," which makes a person forget; *Riddikulus*, which causes things to seem funny; and *Wingardium Leviosa*, "take wings and levitate," which makes people or objects fly through the air.

In *Harry Potter and the Goblet of Fire*, we learn that there are three Unforgivable Curses, and that any wizard who performs them on another human being is liable to lifetime imprisonment at Azkaban. They are *Crucio*, which causes excruciating pain in the victim, *Imperio*, which puts the subject under the wizard's complete command or control, and *Avada Kedavra*, the so-called Killing Curse, which is usually fatal to the subject. It is the *Avada Kedavra* curse that Vordemort employed to destroy Harry's parents, and that he attempts to use on Harry in the cemetery scene in *Harry Potter and the Goblet of Fire*. This curse has a long history of actual usage, and derives from the Aramaic phrase *abhadda kedhabhra*, which means "disappear like this word." It was usually written several times, rather than spoken, in inverted pyramidal form, so that a letter was omitted from each line until the word literally disappeared. The common magician's formula *abra cadabra* was borrowed from this phrase.

Readers will remember that Voldemort also used the *Crucio* formula on Harry in the cemetery scene, and caused Harry to experience extreme pain:

> Voldemort raised his wand, and before Harry could do anything to defend himself, before he could even move, he had been hit again by the Cruciatus Curse. The pain was so intense, so all-consuming, that he no longer knew where he was. . . . White-hot knives were piercing every inch of his skin, his head was surely going to burst with pain, he was screaming more loudly than he'd ever screamed in his life.[2]

Apropos of our discussion of Harry as a Christ figure, there is an obvious connection between the words *Crucio* or *Cruciatus* and *crucifixion*. They are all derived, of course, from the Latin word *crux* or "cross." Crucifixion appears to have been a form of torture invented by the Persians, from whom it passed to the Greeks and Romans. The latter, especially, used it widely throughout their empire as a warning and deterrent to crime, particularly against rebellious slaves and seditious factions in the various provinces. Because it was so terrible, it could not be used on Roman citizens. Always conducted in a public place, it usually included scourging, lashing, or nailing the arms of the victim to a wooden crossbar, an announcement of the person's crime, and slow death by hunger, pain, and exposure. Usually several days were required for persons to die in this manner, and their bodies were left hanging for several more days beyond death, so that people would see them and remember the horror with which they had died. This was considered the most extreme form of death meted out by Roman officials. Jewish historian Josephus called it "the most wretched of deaths." Harry's excruciating pain from Voldemort's curse is consonant with this kind of death, and should underline the possibility that Rowling was thinking about the crucifixion of Jesus when she described his suffering.

THE SOURCES OF ENCHANTMENT

From the sublime to the ridiculous and the serious to the frolicking, there is no question that the reader who enters the fiction of J. K. Rowling is stepping into a world of magic and enchantment, one in which portraits move and talk, trees take out their aggressions on people, ordinary objects fly through the air, strange, belligerent plants, animals, and insects share the planet, and wizards practice exceptional powers that Muggles or ordinary people don't understand and usually don't even see. For young readers, especially, this is part of the fun of a Harry Potter story, and critics who worry that Rowling is trying to herd them into the arms of the occult are probably far more sinister than she. As G. K. Chesteron once said, St. John in his Revelation saw many strange creatures, but none half so strange as some of his interpreters! We ought to remember that Rowling did not invent the world of the extraordinary. On the contrary, she merely stands in the vanguard of numerous writers who have either preceded her or are writing today about such fantastic things that readers must park their common, everyday sense at the door and be prepared for magic and marvel on every hand.

English literature from *Beowulf* to Shakespeare is filled with stories of monsters and supernatural events. The medieval Arthurian legends, stories of King Arthur and the knights of the Round Table, recount numerous battles with strange beasts and people. The fairy tales of both Britain and Europe boast of extraordinary creatures and miraculous powers. Lewis Carroll's *Alice in Wonderland* stories and Frank Baum's *The Wizard of Oz* feature magical settings, extraordinary creatures, talking animals, and animated plants. C. S. Lewis' Narnia tales, which were a favorite of Rowling when she was a child, fairly burst with unbelievable characters and occurrences. J. R. R. Tolkien's *The Hobbits* and *Lord of the Rings* trilogy, other favorites, provide settings and wizards with whom Harry Potter would feel right at home (it is often noted that Dumbledore is extremely similar to Gandalf, the wizard in *Lord of the Rings*). Roald Dahl's *Matilda, The Witches, Charlie and the Chocolate Factory,* and *James and the Giant Peach* all bear striking similarities to the Potter stories.

Elizabeth Schafer, in *Exploring Harry Potter*, lists a number of other works that also foreshadow the Potter oeuvres in noticeable ways: James Barrie's *Peter Pan,* P. L. Travers's *Mary Poppins,* T. H. White's *The Once and Future King,* Ursula LeGuin's *A Wizard of Earthsea,* several of Stephen King's stories, Ian Fleming's *Chitty Chitty Bang Bang: The Magical Car,* Mary Norton's *Bed-knob and Broomstick,* Jane Yolen's *Wizard's Hall, The Pit Dragon* trilogy, and *The Tartan Magic* series, Diane Duane's wizard series, Julie Edwards' *The Last of the Really Great Whangdoodles,* and many other novels and stories too numerous to mention here, including works of both fantasy and science fiction. Clearly, Rowling writes out of a long and respectable tradition of magical worlds.

And, more to our point in this book, what about the wondrous or magical nature of the Bible itself, and Christian history beyond the Bible?

Consider a few of the high points in the Bible. The world is created *ex nihilo* by the spoken fiat of an extraordinarily powerful being named Yahweh or Elohim (the prominent names given in the parallel accounts in the early chapters of Genesis). A woman is created from the rib of a man. A talking serpent beguiles the woman into eating fruit from a forbidden tree. The couple are expelled from Eden for disobedience and a flaming sword is set at the entrance to prevent their return. There are giants in the earth. An invisible divine being speaks audibly to Abraham and tells him he will father a great nation. When Abraham's hand is stayed from sacrificing his son Isaac, a ram is magically provided to take the son's place. Moses encounters a flaming bush that is not consumed. When God sends Moses to free the children of Israel from bondage in

Egypt, he pronounces a number of curses on the Egyptian people, including frogs, flies, locusts, water that turns to blood, boils, and the deaths of firstborn children. As the Israelites flee from the Egyptians, Moses lifts his staff (a wand?) over the sea and the Israelites walk through it on dry land, while the waves engulf the Egyptians behind them. Moses uses the same staff to strike a rock at Horeb and cause drinking water to spout from it. God designates Aaron to assist Moses by making his staff sprout buds, bloom, and bear almonds—all overnight! The prophet Balaam has a conversation with his donkey, which actually talks back. Joshua commands the sun and moon to stand still in their courses until the Israelites have slain all their enemies (did he have a Time-Turner?). The bearers of the Ark of the Covenant stand on dry ground in the middle of the River Jordan before the city of Jericho, and the walls of Jericho collapse as the Israelites march around it, blowing their trumpets.

The angel of God touches Gideon's offering of meat and unleavened cakes with his staff and fire consumes them. As another sign to Gideon, God makes a sheep's wool thick with water, while the ground around it is dry as a bone. A witch at Endor conjures up the dead Samuel for Saul, the king of Israel, and Saul talks with him. Because a widow in Zarephath has been kind to the prophet Elijah, God gives her a jar of meal and a jug of oil that cannot be emptied. Elijah drenches a bull on an altar with water, calls on God, and fire rains on the altar and consumes everything, including the water in the trenches around the altar. Elijah strikes the river with his rolled-up cloak and the water parts so he and Elisha can walk

through on dry ground. Elijah is taken up to heaven in a chariot of fire drawn by horses of fire. Elisha raises a Shunammite
woman's son from death. When a woodsman loses his ax head
in the river, Elisha throws a stick into the water and makes the
ax head float. Isaiah has a dramatic vision of God high on a
throne and surrounded by singing seraphim. Ezekiel is set
down in a valley filled with bones and sees them rise up and
assume their flesh again. Shadrach, Meshach, and Abednego
are thrown into a furnace so hot that it burns the men who
throw them in, but the three survive the heat and are seen
walking around in it with a fourth man; when they emerge, not
even the hair on their heads is singed. The fingers of a human
hand appear and write on the wall in the presence of King Balshazzar. Daniel spends the night untouched in a den of ravenous lions. When Jonah is thrown overboard in a sea storm, he is
swallowed by a great fish, spends three days and nights in the
fish's belly, and is regurgitated on dry land.

All of these stories are in the Old Testament. And what of
the New Testament? Jesus goes everywhere, constantly healing the sick and raising the dead. A woman is cured of a long
illness by touching the hem of his garment. One man he raises
from the dead has been in the tomb for four days and his body
is already rotting. He feeds thousands of people with a handful
of bread and fish. He turns six enormous vats of water into the
finest wine the wine steward ever tasted. He commands sea
storms to cease, and they do. He walks on the sea during a
storm. He casts a legion of demons out of a man and into a
herd of swine, and the swine rush headlong into the sea. He

sends his servants to fetch a coin for taxes from the mouth of a fish. When he is crucified, the sun stops shining for three hours at midday and the graves of Jerusalem open and their dead walk through the city. The women who go to his tomb the third day after his death find it empty and hear from an angel that he has been raised from the dead. He suddenly materializes before his disciples in a room where the doors are locked.

At the Feast of Pentecost, tongues of fire appear on the foreheads of Jesus' followers and they understand languages from all parts of the world (perhaps they would even have understood Parseltongue!). Peter and John heal a man who has been lame from birth. Ananias and Sapphira fall over dead because they lied to the apostles. Saul is struck blind on the road to Damascus and then receives his sight again when touched by another man named Ananias. Peter resuscitates a dead woman named Tabitha. Saul, now called Paul, casts a spell of blindness on a magician named Elymas. A violent earthquake knocks down a prison, freeing Paul and Silas. On the island of Malta, Paul is bitten by a poisonous viper but shakes it off and suffers no ill effects.

These miracles are small compared to some that are reported among the saints of the Middle Ages. For example, St. Basil prayed for a hermit who wished to speak Greek and the man immediately spoke the language perfectly. St. Julian, confronted by a horde of demons in the form of huge Ethiopians, made the sign of the cross and they all disappeared. St. Thomas of Canterbury saw a bird being chased by a hawk. Suddenly it cried out to him, "Saint Thomas, help me!" He prayed for the bird and the hawk fell dead at his feet. When a wolf carried off a poor widow's pig, St. Blaise told her not to be sad, it would be restored to her. Within minutes, the wolf returned and gave the pig to the woman. St. Juliana had molten lead poured over her head, but was unharmed because of her faith. Cast into prison in chains, she was confronted by a demon. Stepping out of the chains, she bound the demon and flogged it with her chains until it cried, "My lady Juliana, have pity on me!"

When a woman laughed at the idea that Christ could be in the bread of the eucharist, St. Gregory prayed and the bread was transformed into a human finger. He prayed again and it was restored to the appearance of bread. The woman instantly became a believer and received communion. In Ireland, a man stole a sheep, cooked it, and ate it. Informed of the theft, St. Patrick called on the thief to come forward. When he didn't, St. Patrick commanded the sheep to bleat in the belly of the man who stole it. When the sheep bleated loudly, the man confessed, accepted his penance, and was restored to the church.

A priest at dinner spoke ill of St. Ambrose, the bishop of Milan. The words were barely out of his mouth when he fell ill, was carried to his bed, and died. St. Theodora revived a dead man who had been mauled by a wild beast. Then she tracked down the beast and cursed it, whereupon it died instantly. St. Margaret was swallowed by an enormous dragon. But she made the sign of the cross from inside it, and immediately it exploded into pieces, setting her free. St. Apollinaris was taken to a temple of the Greek god Apollo and forced to his knees before a statue of the god. He uttered a curse on the statue and it instantly crumbled to pieces.

St. Gregory told his steward to invite twelve pilgrims to dinner. When he saw a thirteenth guest at table, he asked the steward about it. The steward said, "No, my lord, there are only twelve." Taking the thirteenth guest aside, St. Gregory asked the man who he was. "Don't you recognize me, my lord?" he said. "I am the shipwrecked seaman to whom you once gave a silver bowl in which your mother had sent you some vegetables." "How did you know about the vegetables?" asked St. Gregory. "Because I am that seaman's angel," said the man, "and the Lord sent me back so that I might always protect you, and through me you might obtain from him whatever you ask." And immediately the man vanished.

St. Anastasia had three Christian maids who were locked up in a kitchen by a prefect who desired to have sexual relations with them. When he let himself into the kitchen, a spell fell over him, and in his confusion he made love to the stoves, pots, and pans. He came out of the kitchen panting and covered with soot. His servants, who had been waiting outside, thought he was a demon and beat him with rods to drive him away. He went to complain to the emperor, and on his way was set upon by robbers who beat him again, making him blind. Angrier than ever, he had the three maids brought before him and stripped of their clothing, so that his servants could see and describe their beauty to him. But because the maids were under the power of St. Anastasia, their clothing stuck to them like skin and could not be peeled away.

Such stories often grew bigger with the telling, and each province of the Christian world was keen to repeat legends that glorified its own particular saint. Other tales concerned Christians who drove serpents away by making the sign of the cross, preached sermons after all their teeth were knocked out, lived unscathed through hours of burning at the stake, commanded lions, tigers, and elephants to devour their opponents, flew through the heavens like birds, were fed by birds and wild beasts, survived drowning at sea, changed a few crumbs into sumptuous feasts, caused arrows to turn back upon those who shot them, stood up and witnessed after being trampled by horses, brought plagues upon the houses of their enemies, and quoted the entire Bible (including the apochrypha) while standing on one foot!

Are these things wild, or aren't they?

HOW "MAGICAL" IS HARRY POTTER'S WORLD?

The simple fact is, the only newness about Rowling's fictional world is the freshness with which she treats old themes and invents new ones. The world of magic and miracle has been around for a long, long time, and is an intrinsic part of the Judeo-Christian heritage, whatever explanations conservative Christians may wish to offer for it. Rowling herself reminds us of this by the way she intermingles magic and science in the students' curriculum at Hogwarts. "Magic," after all, is related to the word *magi*, the name for those mysterious wise men from the East who came seeking the baby Jesus. They were probably Persian priests who studied the heavens for signs of important events. So the students at Hogwarts study Astrology, among other early sciences, and learn to interpret the influences of the stars and planets. They also study Arithmancy, Herbology, Potions, and a kind of Animal Husbandry that includes strange insects and mythical beasts—all derivatives of ancient sciences with counterparts in modern times.

Rowling's world, in other words, is more whole than a lot of contemporary versions of human existence, for it is more continuous with the real history of understanding as it has developed through the ages. It may also reflect more accurately the nearness of fantasy and fact in modern life—the way a Buck Rogers world actually springs out of the dreams and imaginations of the past. As Arthur C. Clarke, one of the greatest scientific minds of the twentieth century and the man often credited with first envisioning global TV satellites, once said, "Any sufficiently advanced technology is indistinguishable from magic." The reason for this is that skillfully designed technology is basically an outgrowth of the imagination, and *magic* and *imagination* contain the same root meaning. It isn't any wonder that natives who have never seen electric lights, cameras, or television sets regard them as marvels—for, in a way, they are. As Elizabeth Schafer points out, Thomas Edison was known as "the Wizard of Menlo Park" and George Washington Carver was called "the Wizard of Tuskegee."[3]

One of the most provocative books about the nature of reality I have ever read is Lawrence LeShan's *The Medium, the*

Mystic, and the Physicist, first published by Viking Press in 1975. LeShan, a pioneer in paranormal research, explores the relationships among the worlds of clairvoyance, spiritual mysticism, and modern physics, and demonstrates how their territories converge, so that they are actually "three roads to the same reality." We are prone to dismiss single paranormal events as they occur, one by one, because we do not discern any pattern of verifiable relationships among them. The same is true of mystical experiences. But the truth is, says LeShan, that all modern science has sprung from some isolated event or events that spurred the imagination of a curious observer. It is the atypical case, the unusual incident, that, when seriously examined, teaches us about all the others.

It is the one substance in Madame Curie's workshop that glows in the dark that teaches us about the basic structure of all the others. It is the one Petri dish in Fleming's laboratory in which the germs die unexpectedly that leads us to the discovery of the antibiotics. It is the one set of flasks in Pasteur's experiments in which life does *not* appear that teaches us the source of life in the others. It is the atypical paralysis in which neurology can *not* find the lesion that leads Freud to the discovery of the unconscious. It is the one problem in physics (the addition of velocities problem) that cannot be solved in the usual way that leads to an Einsteinian revolution and gives us a deeper understanding of the problems we had been able to solve in the old way.[4]

Proceeding, then, on the premise that we should not dismiss evidences of paranormal occurrences too quickly, without supposing that there must be somewhere a key to the way they are related—albeit too few scientists ever try to find it— LeShan develops his thesis that the basic assumption of all three of his areas of interest, the paranormal, mysticism, and physics, is the *inner unity* of all reality. It is this inner unity that makes their very existence possible. That is, there are *paranormal* occurrences because all psychic phenomena are interrelated and people can be visited by the souls of people from other times and places. Certain persons have *mystical* experiences because either they are preternaturally disposed to be in harmony with invisible spiritual forces or they have learned to position themselves to be receptive to those forces. And the modern physicist believes that the only way to understand the *physical* truths of the universe is to regard them all as interrelated and interdependent, so that time and space and matter must be studied together and not separately.

Is it possible, asks LeShan, that the three worlds and their unities actually overlap? More than that, that they are concentric and coextensive? That reality, far from being the hardheaded, commonsense thing we once believed it to be, is at its core magical and mystical in nature? He cites W. R. Inge, the dean of St. Paul's Cathedral in London, who said in a book called *Christian Mysticism,* "One test is infallible. Whatever view of reality deepens our sense of the tremendous issues of life in the world wherein we move, is for us nearer the truth than any view which diminishes that sense."[5]

The goal of contemporary scientists, like that of both the original scientists and the original religionists, is to provide an understanding of life that is sufficiently broad and unified to describe, not discrete occurrences or experiences, but *everything that is*. As Stephen Hawking, perhaps the most respected theoretical physicist in the world today, says in *A Brief History of Time,* "The eventual goal of science is to provide a single theory that describes the whole universe."[6] Today there are two basic partial theories, the general theory of relativity and quantum mechanics. The first describes the large-scale structure of the universe, from anything the size of a few miles to a million million million million miles, the size of the entire universe; the second deals with phenomena on extremely small scales, such as a millionth of a millionth of an inch. But the two are unfortunately not compatible with each other, which means that one must be wrong. Hawking has said on many occasions that he believes scientists are on the verge of discovering a single theory that will explain everything; and, if that is found, it will answer all the questions that perplex us about not only *how* things work but *why* as well. If we do find that theory, says Hawking at the conclusion of *A Brief History of Time,* it will be "the ultimate triumph of human reason—for then we would know the mind of God."[7]

In view of all this, Harry Potter's world is perhaps not as arbitrary and fantastic as it might appear. Of course it is strange and bizarre. It is a hodgepodge of magic, dreams, and imagination, and constantly assaults the boundaries of credibility. But many of its weird practices and ideas are no wilder than those of ancient and medieval science—or, for that matter, some of the practices and ideas of a considerably more recent science, in, say, Newtonian physics or twentieth-century medicine. In other words, the fact that we have not yet arrived at a unified understanding of the world and how things work and what they mean does much to legitimize the fantastical approach of a Tolkien or a Dahl or a Rowling; the world as they describe it is in some ways as warrantable as any other partial view of life in the universe.

What the magical, mystical world of an Alice, a Frodo, or a Harry Potter does do for us is remind us of how exciting it is to live in a universe where we are still discovering things, where the absolutely worst thing that can happen to us is to surrender to the dementors and become soulless, mirthless beings staggering around amid all this beauty and wonder. As Schafer says:

> Magic seems to be an intrinsic part of human behavior. Humans want to be tricked and astounded so that they can question the natural order of their world and their basic beliefs. As society has become more industrialized and reliant on technology, many people sense their community has been demythologized, or stripped of mystery and wonder, and they feel empty. Magic helps fill their spirits with a sense of surprise, astonishment, and bewilderment about their external surroundings and internal self.[8]

A REKINDLING OF SPIRITUAL CONSCIOUSNESS

Nowhere in modern literature is this recovery of "surprise, astonishment, and bewilderment" more talked about than in the writings of Christian spiritualists. The spiritual tradition in Christianity has very ancient and venerable roots, of course, going all the way back to the *Confessions* of St. Augustine. It reemerged with power in the writings of Ignatius of Loyola, Teresa of Avila, and John of the Cross in the sixteenth century; and it has continued to be a phenomenon more Catholic than Protestant through Thomas Merton in the midtwentieth century. As the popularity of Asian studies, especially Buddhism, grew in America during the time of the Vietnam War, it merged with a general admiration of Merton to produce a new, widespread fascination with the idea of spirituality as an almost transreligious experience. While Christianity bought into the fascination with hundreds of books and conferences on the so-called Jesus prayer and a specifically Christian content to spirituality, there continues to be a vast secular interest in what it means to be a finely tuned, sensitively adjusted human being who is open to the divine currents in the galaxy and indeed regards the fulfillment of human nature as something virtually impossible apart from such an alignment with higher forces.

One exemplar of this "higher consciousness" is a woman named Julia Butterfly Hill, who in her twenties spent two years living in an ancient redwood tree in Northern California to prevent the Pacific Lumber Company from cutting down the tree for lumber. She gave the tree a name—Luna—and later called her autobiography *The Legacy of Luna*. Charles Hurwitz, chairman of the corporation that owned Pacific Lumber, spent hours trying to talk Hill out of the tree. He threatened to take her to court and have her removed from the forest. Hill believed she was serving the power of love in the world, and prayed to the "Universal Spirit" to give her the strength to serve it by protecting the wonderful tree. Eventually, she and Pacific Lumber Company reached an accord that was supposed to spare the tree, although the company later found a way to proceed with its logging operations in the area.

Many people did not understand Hill's devotion to the redwood. Spending so many months of her young life in a tree, they thought, was crazy. They said she was right to call the tree Luna, because she herself was displaying signs of lunacy. But Hill became a heroine to the real spiritualists of the age because she represented a sensitivity to all life they were seeking for themselves. Like the Buddhists of the 1970s who set themselves aflame for world peace, she was prepared to sacrifice herself for the good of the whole, for the sacredness of life itself.

Matthew Fox, the controversial Catholic priest who became an Episcopalian when his bishop refused to let him continue saying Mass, says in the introduction of his book *One River, Many Wells*:

> My thoughts turn to the subject of our various religions. None of them is mother of the ocean, rather the ocean is mother of all things. Our religions are so recent in relation

to the lifetime of the sea and to most other creatures—
including humanity itself. What religions did our ancestors
practice for the two million years that preceded the forms
we now recognize as 'world religions'? How humble our
religions ought to be before all creatures. As Mechtild of
Magdeburg said, 'the truly wise person kneels at the feet of
all creatures.'[9]

Maybe this is why, as Schafer notes, the Christian holidays
in the Potter stories—Halloween, Christmas, and Easter—
have become secularized and are not treated from a Christian
perspective at all. They reflect the reality of the new global
society in which, for many people, attachment to a particular
religious faith has been superseded by a more generalized spirituality in which people are no longer divided from one
another by the walls of sectarianism. The old holidays remain,
but as vestiges of a particularized, sectarian faith, and the new
ones have not yet emerged. One suspects that eventually they
will—Earth Day and Global Awareness Day and Love Day and
Isn't It Good to Be Alive Day.

Writer Anne Lamott describes the new spirit in her book
Traveling Mercies when she talks about why she makes her little son Sam go to church with her even though he hates to get
cleaned up and go:

> The main reason is that I want to give him what I found
> in the world, which is to say a path and a little light to see by.
> Most of the people I know who have what I want—which is

to say, purpose, heart, balance, gratitude, joy—are people with a deep sense of spirituality. They are people in community, who pray, or practice their faith; they are Buddhists, Jews, Christians—people banding together to work on themselves and for human rights. They follow a brighter light than the glimmer of their own candle; they are part of something beautiful.[10]

Most of the students and faculty at Hogwarts School of Witchcraft and Wizardry would understand this. They feel this sense of community, of following "a brighter light than the glimmer of their own candle," in their assemblages in the Great Hall, especially at beginnings and ends of terms. The Slytherins appear to feel it least, for they belong to a tradition inaugurated by Salazar Slytherin, who was devoted to the Dark Arts, and are less open to other ways. But the other students and faculty, particularly the Gryffindors, gather in a sense of unity and joy, and their celebration of Harry's victories is at least a little like the celebration at Christian communion of the victory of Christ.

As I have commented before, it is no accident that the position Harry Potter plays on the Gryffindors' Quidditch team is that of Seeker, for that is the title given to those in our time who seek this higher sense of the spiritual in their lives, who wish especially to remain open and attentive to the wonder and beauty of human existence. Wonder, in any religious tradition, lies at the heart of its sense of discovery and worship. What did Dag Hammarskjöld, the popular

United Nations secretary general who died in a plane crash, write in his diary?

> God does not die on the day when we cease to believe
> in a personal deity, but we die on the day when our lives
> cease to be illumined by the steady radiance, renewed daily,
> of a wonder, the source of which is beyond all reason.[11]

A distinguished Brit, Michael Mayne, who was dean of Westminster in London, wrote a book called *This Sunrise of Wonder,* which is filled with a vibrant and delicate sensitivity to the life of the world around him. He went to Switzerland to write the book, and penned it as a series of letters to his grandchildren, to remind them of the importance of being attentive to their rich environment. Early on, he says, "My subject is wonder, and my starting point so obvious it often escapes us. It is me, sitting at a table looking out on the world. It is the fact that I exist, that there is anything at all. It is the *givenness* that astonishes: the fact that the mountains, the larch tree, the gentian, the jay, *exist,* and that someone called *me* is here to observe them."[12] Later, he cites Meister Eckhardt, the medieval mystic, who wrote of how each of us must discover "our own ground," so that little by little we begin to detach ourselves from our egos and reflect the divine purpose at the center of all life. "That suggests," says Mayne, "that the deepest mystery about me is that I can find God in the depths of myself; and having begun to do so I am then enabled to find him everywhere."[13]

Givenness—haecceity—quidditas. The *this*ness or *what*-ness or particularity of things, of every thing, that participates finally—had we but the vision and understanding to perceive it—in the unity of the ALL, so that there is at last wonder and marvel in everything, breathing and nonbreathing, in the universe. It is this to which Rowling's world of magic and mysticism witnesses, this which she invites us to see by showing us talking portraits and exploding candies and almost-headless ghosts and ugly trolls and nipping hippogriffs. And if we don't see—*can't see*—then we are unfortunately like the Muggles in her stories, who live drably in everyday surroundings without ever knowing about the real color and magic and adventure around them. We are like the Dursley family, whose greatest concerns are for generous-sized slabs of breakfast bacon and vacations in Majorca and making a good impression on Mr. Dursley's boss.

OF GHOSTS AND GOBLINS
AND THE LIFE AFTER DEATH

CHAP. 5.

BELIEVE IN . . . the resurrection of the body, and the life everlasting." Millions of Christians repeat these words from the Apostles' Creed every week in their services of worship. Not all of them believe the words, of course. Bryant Kirkland, long-time minister of Fifth Avenue Presbyterian Church in New York City, loved to tell about the slightly inebriated parishioner who phoned him one night to say she was at a party where several of her friends were animatedly discussing what they believed, and, embarrassed by her inability to join in, she wanted to know, "Doctor, what is it exactly that we Presbyterians believe?" But belief in the resurrection and everlasting life has been a cardinal tenet of the Christian church since the days of the apostles themselves. Christianity simply would not be Christianity were it denuded of this doctrine.

Yet in recent years it has become harder and harder for the average Christian to accept life after death as a fact, or even a reasonably sure bet. The more urban and technological the globe has become, and the more impersonal its parishes, the more difficult it has been to think of mortality with any sense of triumph, the way Christians usually did in previous eras. The Bible calls death "the last enemy"—sort of like Lord Voldemort, whose name is so appropriate—and the majority of Christians today probably agree with that assessment without experiencing any consolation of faith in eternal life. Just as most of the wizards in the Potter stories prefer not to have Voldemort actually named in conversation, but refer to him as You-Know-Who, most people today avoid really facing the fact of death, which is personally quite threatening, and support a collective effort to disguise it with cosmetics, canned music, and canapes. We are much more subdued and evasive at funerals than we are at cocktail parties.

Two hundred fifty years ago, Jonathan Edwards, now regarded as the finest preacher in eighteenth-century America, assaulted his congregation with constant remembrances of their mortality, and spoke in the most graphic terms of the kind of afterlife awaiting them. Today, from the staid old sanctuaries of Boston and New York to the hip churches of the California coast, death is seldom mentioned, and it is a rare preacher indeed who dares to speculate about the nature of the soul's survival after death. Surveys have shown that even on Easter, the Day of Resurrection, when it would be most natural for clergy to tackle the subject of an afterlife, most of them demur, preferring to talk instead about the beauties of nature or the importance of a life of faith.

In light of this absence of plain talk about death, readers ought to be happy with the prominence J. K. Rowling assigns to the interaction between the living and the dead, and the way her wizards are never fully separated from those who have died. Her novels are peopled by ghosts, goblins, and poltergeists as well as living persons, and the members of the Hogwarts community, who represent the more sensitive and understanding element of the British populace, accept these spectral presences as matter-of-factly as they do the presence of one another. Interestingly, the subject of death never comes up in the Dursley household, and we can guess without any trouble what the Dursleys' reactions would be if it did. They are like the majority of people in our own world who shun the topic of mortality as completely as possible, while the wizards at Hogwarts, who are far more in the know about things, deal with it in every story.

It is all related, in a sense, to the openness to wonder we considered in the last chapter. Life and death are part of the magic of the universe, but we understand this only as we draw aside from the hurly-burly of our busy existence and learn to marvel at everything. Macrina Wiederkehr puts it beautifully in her book *A Tree Full of Angels:*

> Spending your days in the fast lane of life impairs the quality of your seeing. If you want to see to the depths, you will need to slow down. You live in a world of theophanies. Holiness comes wrapped in the ordinary. There are burning bushes all around you. Every tree is full of angels. Hidden

beauty is waiting in every crumb. Life wants to lead you from crumbs to angels, but this can happen only if you are willing to unwrap the ordinary by staying with it long enough to harvest its treasure.[1]

THE THIN LINE

J. K. Rowling treats death as a reality—a *harsh* reality that separates families from loved ones. Her mother died of multiple sclerosis while she was still revising her first novel, and she has said that it had an enormous impact on her. Harry Potter lives with sadness and regret for the parents he barely knows, and Cedric Diggory's family, in *Harry Potter and the Goblet of Fire,* is truly grief-stricken when Cedric is murdered by Voldemort. Yet Rowling also treats the dead as if they are never all that far from the living, as if a very thin line divides the realms of the mortal and immortal. Her novels are peopled by innumerable ghosts as well as living creatures, and for the wizards, who are more sensitive to these matters than Muggles are, there is often some form of communication with them.

Rowling distinguishes between three kinds of spirits: ghosts, goblins, and poltergeists. The most prominent ghosts are Sir Nicholas de Mimsy-Porpington, also called Nearly Headless Nick, the resident ghost of Gryffindor Tower, who can seize his ear, pull off his once nearly decapitated head, and lay it on his shoulder; and Moaning Myrtle, who was murdered in one of the women's bathrooms and continues to live there, although she appears in other places, too. The best known of the poltergeists is Peeves, an irascible spirit (hence his name) who behaves like a spoiled child, throwing food at the table, playing practical jokes on students, messing up the halls, and generally making a nuisance of himself. But these are only the best known of countless spirits who inhabit the premises of Hogwarts.

Harry, along with other first-year students, is startled at his initial encounter with them:

> He gasped. So did the people around him. About twenty ghosts had just streamed through the back wall. Pearly-white and slightly transparent, they glided across the room talking to one another and hardly glancing at the first years. They seemed to be arguing. What looked like a fat little monk was saying: "Forgive and forget, I say, we ought to give him a second chance—"[2]

The ghosts are often seen frequenting the halls this way, and apparently are always present in the Great Hall for meals and festivities. In *Harry Potter and the Chamber of Secrets*, Harry and Nearly Headless Nick are walking together in the hall, when Nick suddenly stops and Harry walks right through him. He wishes he hadn't, for it feels "like stepping through an icy shower." Nick has just thought to invite Harry and his friends to his five-hundredth "deathday party," which will be held on Halloween in one of the roomier dungeons.

As Harry, Ron, and Hermione approach the party, they

almost wish they hadn't promised to attend. The way is lit by black tapers that cast a dim, hazy light over everything. When they enter the dungeon, they see hundreds of pearly, translucent figures drifting around a crowded dance floor, waltzing to "the dreadful, quavering sound of thirty musical saws." The youngsters' breath hovers visibly in the air. They feel as if they are standing in a freezer. The food table, covered with such revolting "delicacies" as maggoty haggis, furry green cheese, and rotten fish, bears a large gray cake resembling a tombstone. An inscription on the cake, in tarlike icing, says:

SIR NICHOLAS DE MIMSY-PORPINGTON
DIED 31ST OCTOBER, 1492

Later, as Nick is about to notify the orchestra and start the speech he has prepared for the occasion, the party is interrupted by the sound of a hunting horn. A dozen ghost horses, each ridden by a headless horseman, clatter onto the scene. The lead horseman, a ghost named Sir Patrick, leaps down, holds his head aloft, and taunts Nick about his still partly attached head. And when Nick mounts the podium and attempts to give his speech, he is interrupted again by Sir Patrick and his friends, who have just started a game of Head Hockey, causing the audience to follow the movement of the head and lose all interest in Nick.

This is rollicking good fun—no one doubts Rowling's sense of humor—but is it justifiable treatment of the dead? American readers, especially, have to remember the long and varied history of ghosts and ghost behavior in Great Britain, where numerous houses, hotels, and public buildings are reputedly inhabited by deceased spirits and there are many stories about the humorous idiosyncrasies of some of them. If people were inclined to be noisy, boisterous, or sportive in life, their shadows are often likely to reflect those characteristics in the afterlife.

Rowling follows this boisterous scene with Harry's hearing, for the second time, the strange voice he heard earlier in Professor Lockhart's office, growling, "... *rip* ... *tear* ... *kill*." It will turn out to be the voice of the basilisk from the hidden chamber, controlled by Voldemort, although Harry, who speaks Parseltongue, is the only one who actually hears discernible words. The effect of turning from the hilarity of Nearly Headless Nick's party to this chilling reminder of the presence of evil is little short of stunning! It says, in essence, that we live in a very spiritual universe where some spirits are benign and others are dark and threatening, and sensitive people, who are aware of both, will often careen wildly between them.

The ghosts apparently lead parallel lives with the students and faculty, discussing school events and even maintaining their old house loyalties. In *Harry Potter and the Goblet of Fire*, Harry and his friends are sitting by Nearly Headless Nick at the opening banquet of the school year, when the Sorting Hat decides which houses the new students will join. Nick belongs to Gryffindor House, while another ghost, the Bloody Baron, is a Slytherin. Nick and the Baron are discussing a recent ghosts' council meeting in which the topic of Peeves' antisocial behavior was hotly debated. Peeves has been wreaking havoc in the kitchen, hurling pots and pans everywhere, inundating the place with soup, and terrifying the house-elves out of their wits. Harry, Ron, and Hermione enter the conversation as naturally as if there were no distinction between them and the ghosts, the living and the dead.

Many writers on the subject of life after death stress the incredible nearness of the dead, especially the recently dead, to those who are living. Edgar Cayce, the American spiritualist, wrote many times of cases in which he experienced the presence of dead persons with messages for the living. Hans Holzer, whose *Life After Death: The Challenge and the Evidence* was one of the first immensely popular books in the genre, insists that the dead continue to move among us, not only attempting to communicate with us but actually relocating objects and interfering in our actions to affect the decisions we make. Moreover, he says, it isn't merely the deceased with whom we have had close emotional ties who try to contact us or interface with our lives. Sometimes it is distant relatives or persons we didn't even know—friends of friends, so to speak, who are part of a network of spirits on the other side.

When Bishop James Pike's son died from a fall in New York City, Pike, who up to that time was a very practical, hardheaded realist who had nothing to do with spiritualism, began consulting mediums in the attempt to contact the boy. Convinced that he and his son did have several conversations with the assistance of mediums, he wrote a book called *The Other*

Side. Once, he said, his son told him about meeting Paul Tillich on the other side. Tillich, the leading existential theologian of the twentieth century, whom Pike had known but his son had not, gave the boy a characteristic message to pass on to his father. This convinced Pike that spirits of the dead continue to monitor our thoughts and actions and to care about what we do.

Is Rowling flouting any Christian understanding of life after death with her fun-loving accounts of ghosts at Hogwarts? Not really, because there isn't any orthodox viewpoint about the nature of life after death. Among Christians, there is only the insistence that life after death exists, and beyond that there is little agreement about what it might entail. In fact, today there is very little discussion of the matter at all. Theologians sometimes argue over the question of "soul-sleeping"— whether references in the Bible to the thousand-year reign of Christ before the final judgment mean that there will be no resurrection of the dead until then and they remain meanwhile in a state of suspended animation. And Oscar Cullmann wrote an engaging study a few years ago, called *Immortality of the Soul or Resurrection of the Dead?*, in which he drew a careful distinction between the Greek notion of general immortality and the Hebrew-Christian idea of the individual's being raised by God, the latter concept recognizing divine sovereignty in the matter. But on the whole there is a kind of acceptable pandemonium regarding the subject. Beyond the agreement that the church should retain the assertion about resurrection of the body and life everlasting in its creed, there is very little official superintendence over exactly what we do believe about life after death.

THE MEMORY OF THE DEAD

Rowling flirts with one curious idea in her treatment of the dead, and that is the relationship between a ghost and a memory. It occurs in Harry's confrontation with Tom Riddle, a.k.a. Voldemort, in the Chamber of Secrets below Hogwarts. Tom, whose full name, Tom Marvolo Riddle, is an anagram for "I am Lord Voldemort," was a student at Hogwarts fifty years earlier; it is his diary with which Harry has been conversing for a number of weeks. Yet when Harry finally encounters him in the chamber, he looks the way he did fifty years ago, as though he were only sixteen.

"Are you a ghost?" asks Harry, uncertainly.

"A memory," says Riddle quietly. "Preserved in a diary for fifty years."[3]

Harry's friend, Ginny Weasley, found the diary and had been writing in it for months, pouring out her innermost secrets to Riddle. Now he has used those accumulated secrets, the strength of Ginny's life, to reassemble himself and leave the pages of the diary, and he stands before Harry as the embodiment not just of Tom Riddle but of Lord Voldemort himself. As we shall discover again in *Harry Potter and the Goblet of Fire*, the evil Lord Voldemort depends on the strength of others for his own vitality.

Is there any significance to Riddle's comment that he is a "memory" and not a "ghost"? Does he mean that the student Tom Riddle is only a memory because he is now actually Voldemort? Or is there a valid distinction between being a memory and being a ghost?

Common imagination suggests that a ghost is a more collected, vital entity than a memory. That is, a memory is scattered, fleeting, part of a generalized mosaic of impressions we bear of someone who died, while a ghost is a more specific, gathered impression, even a personality that continues to exist with some force, albeit diminished from that of the original. Christians hold services in memory of the dead. All Saints' Day is a specific occasion each year when honor and reverence are paid to those who have died, and Memorial Day exists to pay homage to those who died in military service for their country. But the appearance of an actual ghost, on either of those occasions, would prove extremely unsettling to those merely "remembering" the dead.

Michael Mayne, in *This Sunrise of Wonder*, offers a fascinating thought about remembering people and things. He is writing to his grandchildren, as we have noted before, and discusses the mystery of memory—specifically how the hippocampus, which is thought to be the residence of memory in the human brain, is related to the reality of daily life.

In *Moon Tiger* by Penelope Lively, the 67-year-old Caludia [sic], smelling eucalyptus leaves in post-war Cairo, is overwhelmed by

> *wonder that nothing is ever lost, that everything can be*
> *retrieved, that a lifetime is not linear but instant. That,*
> *inside the head, everything happens at once.*

That takes us again to the heart of the mystery. One day, when you are looking back on your lives, you will find that all the people you have ever been (and we play many parts), all the bodies you have worn, all the faces of people and the look of places you have loved, still live inside your skin; they are still lodged in that part of your brain that is the memory.[4]

Perhaps if there were really such a device as the Time-Turner which Hermione used in *Harry Potter and the Prisoner of Azkaban* to reverse the hours so she can attend two classes that meet at the same time, and then by Harry and Hermione to turn back the clock long enough to rescue Sirius Black from the tower before the executioner can reach him, it would bear a key relationship to this philosophical question. It would make it possible for us to revisit our memories when they were at their most forceful, in their original existence.

But is a memory really less powerful than the thing it recalls? We generally assume it is. Yet what if the memory becomes a powerful motivation in real life? Suppose, for example, the recollection of Todd Beamer, one of the passengers on United Airlines flight 93 that was hijacked and crashed on September 11, 2001, inspires millions of people to live their lives more sacrificially and to give vast sums of money to various service organizations. Could Beamer possibly have had such influence while he was alive? Memories are not the same thing as ghosts, certainly. But they are obviously forceful in their own way.

Harry Potter's parents are both memories and ghosts in his life. He cherishes everything he can learn about them, because he was too young to remember them before they were killed, and he depends on the descriptions of Hagrid, Dumbledore, Sirius Black, Professor Lupin, and others to assemble memories that will surely influence him all his life. But his parents also appear to him as definable personalities—first in the Mirror of Erised, in *Harry Potter and the Sorcerer's Stone,* and then in freer, more "real" encounters—and he interacts with them not as memories but as living beings.

The whole question of the relationship of memory to life, merely touched on by Rowling, suggests Einstein's idea of relativity and the pursuit of theoretical physicists today for a unified theory of matter. If time is not linear, as we tend to presume, but is somehow cyclical or telescoped, so that all things happen coevally even though we perceive them as individuated, then there is a far more intimate relationship than we usually imagine between memory and reality. And it is all part of the sheer wonder of existence, the magic of being, that we touched on in the last chapter. Rowling is a mistress of wonder. It is her stock in trade, so to speak, and she may well have dropped the hint about memory and ghosts merely to provoke our speculation.

She has confessed that Elizabeth Goudge is one of her favorite writers, so she is doubtless aware of this passage from

Pilgrim's Inn where Jill and her twin children have followed an old familiar path through the woods in search of Christmas holly:

> When she had filled her basket with holly Jill sat down on the rock and waited happily for the twins. She did not find the waiting irksome, for she had been born one of those fortunate people who are never in a hurry and never restless. She had never felt restless in her life. In all that she did, in all that she saw, she was aware of a deep upspringing wonder, as though she did it or saw it for the first time. She was blessed with a mind neither retrospective nor anxious; the past and the future did not pull her two ways with remorse and dread, and the lovely freshness of each new-made moment was apparent to her focused vision.[5]

By her own confession, Rowling is often filled with anxiety, especially about getting her writing done. But, like Jill, she is "aware of a deep upspringing wonder," and her "focused vision" is able to hold both past and present in easy suspension, so that memories are real life and real life is already in the process of becoming memories.

RECOGNITION OF THE DEAD

The Christian faith has always alternated between the belief that those who have died have gone to be with the Lord—

really *gone*—and the belief that they remain somehow in the vicinity of the living, at least part of the time, and continue to reveal themselves to the people who mattered to them. John Calvin, for example, whose *Institutes* is one of the most formidable treatises on the church and its faith ever written, held that it is the sovereignty of God that is most important in the discussion of any tenet of faith, and was therefore ill disposed to consider that souls remain in any personal relationship with those they have left behind; their business in the afterlife is merely to join the chorus of saints who sing constant praises to the deity. Popular experience, however, appears to weigh heavily on the other side, and many Christian thinkers are of the firm opinion that the dead not only remain accessible to the living but are instantly recognizable to them.

Here, for example, is a passage from Leslie D. Weatherhead's popular *The Christian Agnostic,* which was published as Weatherhead's summa after his years as a well-known minister in London during and following World War II:

> As the last shadows fall, again and again the watcher by the bedside will see a strange, new light in eyes now opening easily, and the expression of those eyes is one of supreme joy and happiness. Then, in a way almost startling, the patient will sit up—he who could not raise his head—stretch out his arms and call the name of a beloved, dead it may be, a score of years before.
>
> My beloved father-in-law, when dying, was sure that a

daughter who had been dead for years was with him in his bedroom. Some of my own experiences in the death-chamber support this conclusion. Rosalind Heywood, watching a dying man, saw him suddenly sit up. She writes, "His face lit up. 'It's Annie,' he cried, gazing in joyous recognition at someone I could not see, 'And John! . . . Oh the Light! the Light!' "

If that is a trick of the patient's brain or nervous system, if it is the hallucination of a disordered mind, all I can say is that it is strangely convincing to the watcher. Having seen that more than once, I for one am in no doubt about man's survival of death or of his reunion with those he loves.[6]

Weatherhead's conclusion is supported by mountains of evidence from students of the life-after-life experience, such as Dr. Raymond Moody (*Life After Life* and *Reflections on Life After Life*), Dr. Maurice Rawlings (*Beyond Death's Door*), and Drs. Karlis Osis and Erlendur Haraldsson (*At the Hour of Death*). The well-known priest, sociologist, and writer Andrew Greeley tells in *Death and Beyond* about a poll of almost fifteen hundred persons he conducted in 1974, in which one of the questions was: "Have you ever felt that you were really in touch with someone who had died?" More than 25 percent of those asked testified that they had had such an experience, half of these more than once or several times. Among persons over the age of seventy, 39 percent had had the experience. A similar poll conducted two years later in Great Britain showed very similar results.

There is also biblical evidence behind this view. In the Old Testament, when King Saul consults the medium of Endor and bids her to summon the deceased prophet Samuel for him, both she and Saul recognize the old man who emerges from the ground, his robe pulled around him.[7] When Jesus appears to the disciples in the upper room following his crucifixion, and again at the Sea of Galilee where they are fishing, they know him.[8] The two disciples traveling to Emmaus do not recognize him immediately, but finally realize who he is as they are breaking bread together.[9] And the Apostle Paul, delivering the *kerygma,* or essentials, of the faith commonly held in the early church, refers to the occasion when more than five hundred people were with Christ and recognized him.[10]

There is no speculation in the Potter novels about where people go after death or what their afterlife experiences are like. But the dead are very certainly recognizable to the living, and continue to manifest essentially the same personalities they had in life. Nearly Headless Nick still appears in courtly dress and behaves very much as he did when he was a knightly warrior, although he has been dead half a millennium. James and Lily Potter are essentially as they were in life and continue to show parental interest in their son. And Professor Binns, the professor of the History of Magic whom we meet in *Harry Potter and the Chamber of Secrets,* is actually a ghost who has gone on teaching. As Rowling says, the most exciting thing about Binns' rather dull classes is that he enters the room through the blackboard. Because he was an ancient and shriveled man for many years, some people admit they hadn't even noticed he was dead. He simply got up to teach one day and left his body sitting in an armchair in front of the staff-room fire, and his routine has not varied an iota since.

Near the end of *Harry Potter and the Prisoner of Azkaban,* when Harry and Dumbledore are having the conversation that helps Harry to understand and come to terms with all that has transpired, Harry talks about the Patronus in the form of a stag that saved him from the dementors. Harry says he thought it was his father who had conjured the Patronus. "I mean, when I saw myself across the lake . . . I thought I was seeing him." Dumbledore says it was an easy mistake to make, because Harry does look amazingly like his father.

Harry shakes his head and says it was stupid of him to think it was his dad. "I mean, I knew he was dead."

"You think the dead we loved ever truly leave us?" asks Dumbledore. "You think that we don't recall them more clearly than ever in times of great trouble? Your father is alive in you, Harry, and shows himself most plainly when you have need of him. How else could you produce that *particular* Patronus? Prongs rode again last night."[11]

IN AID OF THE LIVING

This brings us to another point of the discussion, and an important one for many Christians: That the dead not only continue to have an existence of some kind but actually intervene in our affairs to help us when we need them. Apart from the work of

Christ himself, and an image in the Apocalypse of the saints in heaven praying for the souls of the living, there is not any biblical warrant for the opinion that the dead actively assist the living. But there is no doubt at all in popular Christianity that those who have died are valuable allies to the living. The idea of applying to the saints for assistance probably had its origin in praying for Christ's intercession, then Mary's, and finally that of other holy persons. Claudius, the ninth-century bishop of Turin, vigorously opposed the saying of prayers to the dead, but history took little notice of him. The idea that those who have already died can help us in our continuing struggle in this earthly existence is deeply enmeshed in all the Christian traditions—Roman Catholic, Orthodox, and even Protestant. Most saints have become particularly identified with different kinds of needs—Christopher is the patron saint of travelers; Anthony of Padua, Martin of Tours, and Vincent de Paul are patron saints of horses, and Brigid, Drogo, and Perpetua, of cows; Brendan, of whales; Ursula, Gregory the Great, and Catherine of Alexandria, of teachers; Angela and Gerard, of mentally or physically challenged persons; Anne and Anthony of Pavoni, of people who have lost things; Luke, Damian, and Pantaleon, of doctors; Catherine and Genesius, of secretaries; and Matthew, of security guards. Saint Paul the Apostle is the patron saint of poisonous snakes. But most Christians believe that even a godly parent, godparent, aunt, uncle, teacher, or acquaintance is a valuable friend in the life beyond.

J. K. Rowling appears firm in this belief as well. Moaning Myrtle is a good example. We first meet Myrtle in *Harry Potter and the Chamber of Secrets,* when Hermione confesses to Harry and Ron that she doesn't like to use the girls toilet where Myrtle lives because she is always "having tantrums and flooding the place." It is through Myrtle that Harry first discovers the diary of Tom Riddle and later realizes that the way to the secret chamber under the school must lie through her bathroom. When he asks her how she died, she isn't really certain. She remembers that she was in the toilet, hiding because another girl had been teasing her about her glasses, when she heard a boy's voice speaking a language she didn't understand. She unlocked the door and came out to tell him to use the boys toilet, when she suddenly died. The only thing she recalls about it is that she saw "a pair of great, big, yellow eyes"—those of the basilisk. Harry, Ron, and Professor Lockhart, the latter unwillingly, find the bathroom entrance to the basilisk's chambers below and descend there to face Voldemort and the mythical beast.

In *Harry Potter and the Goblet of Fire,* Myrtle appears to Harry out of one of the water taps when he is taking a bath in the prefect's room and trying to figure out the secret of the golden egg for the second task in the Triwizard Tournament. She complains that he hasn't been to see her lately—an indication that she likes him—and he says he was reprimanded for going to the women's toilet. She tells him to try putting the egg underwater—that that is what Cedric Diggory did that led him to its secret. He lowers the egg, but hears only a gurgling sound. "You need to put your head under too," she urges. "Go on!"[12] Harry submerges himself three times, until he has memorized the song being sung by the egg, but he still doesn't understand. So Myrtle chats with him about the clue until he figures out that the task is to rescue someone or something he will miss from the merpeople beneath the lake. When he leaves the bathroom, Myrtle asks him if he will come and visit her again in her bathroom, and he says he'll try.

Harry encounters Myrtle again under the lake when he is trying to find the village of the merpeople. He has just encountered a band of grindylows and managed to extricate himself from them when he hears her speak to him. He tries to speak too, but can only manage a bubble out of his mouth, which amuses Myrtle. "You want to try over there," she says, pointing. "I won't come with you. . . . I don't like them much, they always chase me when I get too close. . . ."[13] Harry follows her directions, and soon finds himself among the merpeople and their captives. So once more Myrtle has helped Harry in his competition for the Triwizard Cup.

But it is Harry's deceased parents who are his most persistent helpers. Even in death, they continue the kind of love and concern for his welfare that marked their attempt to protect him when they were murdered by Voldemort.

Harry first gets sight of them in the Mirror of Erised, in *Harry Potter and the Sorcerer's Stone*. As he looks into the magical mirror, he sees a crowd of people standing behind him. He whirls around, but the room is empty. He looks again. There are at least ten people standing behind him. Are they really in the room with him, but invisible? Or are they in the mirror? He looks again. There is a woman standing immediately behind his reflection, and she is smiling and waving at him. She is a pretty woman, with green eyes that look exactly like his. He notices that she is crying—smiling and crying at the same time. And behind her stands a tall, thin, black-haired man who wears glasses and whose hair is untidy and sticks up in the back just like Harry's.

Harry is so close to the mirror now that his nose is almost touching it. "Mom?" he whispers. "Dad?"

He looks at the other people in the group behind him. There are other pairs of green eyes like his, other noses like his, even a little old man who appears to have his own knobbly knees. Harry is looking at his family. He remains standing there a long time, staring at them. When he finally tears himself away to return to bed, he whispers, "I'll come back."[14]

In *Harry Potter and the Prisoner of Azkaban*, Professor Lupin, the Defense Against the Dark Arts teacher, shows Harry how to summon a Patronus, or guardian spirit, to scatter the boggarts that attack one and cause depression. Boggarts are called "shape-shifters" because they change their appearance to assume the shape of whatever the viewer fears most. For Harry, the shape they assume is that of the dementors, the hideous creatures from Azkaban that suck the souls out of the prisoners. When Harry asks what a Patronus will look like if he manages to accomplish the spell Professor Lupin is teaching him, Lupin says it is always unique to the boggart. And in Harry's case, when he pronounces the spell *"Expecto patronum!"* he at first hears loud voices shouting, and realizes they are his parents' voices as they try to fend off Voldemort and save Harry's life. Then, out of a white fog, his Patronus appears. It is a huge, silver shadow that comes between him and the boggart, forcing the boggart to retreat. Later in the same novel, when Lupin has turned into a werewolf, Harry looks across the lake and sees a great crowd of dementors, at least a hundred of them, gliding around the lake in his direction.

"Expecto patronum!" he shouts. *"Expecto patronum!"*

He shouts it again and again. For a moment, a silver mist arises between him and the nearest dementor. Then the dementor lowers its hood and he can see its eyeless face with its scabby, gray skin, and its mouth, a gaping, shapeless hole, sucking in air with the sound of a death rattle. His Patronus flickers and disappears. He tries again to summon it, but feels strong, clammy hands around his neck. He can hear his mother's voice screaming in his ears, as he must have when he was a baby and she was trying to save him from Voldemort. He seems to be drowning in fog. Then a silvery light grows brighter and brighter, and he realizes that the dementor has released him. He is too weak to stand, but he looks around. Something is driving the dementors away. It is circling him. With every ounce of strength he can muster, he lifts his head in time to see a great silver animal amid the light, galloping away across the lake. It returns to someone there, and someone is patting it, as if to say it has done a good job.

When Harry discusses it all with Hermione, she wants to know who conjured the Patronus. Harry thinks about it and realizes who he *thought* it was. "I think—" he says, hesitantly, knowing it will sound strange to her, "I think it was my dad." Hermione reminds him that his father is dead. He says he knows it. She wants to know if it was his father's ghost. "I don't know," he says, ". . . no . . . he looked solid. . . ."[15]

Later, near Hagrid's cottage by the Forbidden Forest, he hears yelping in the distance and knows the dementors are closing in on Sirius Black, who has transformed himself into the big black dog. In a minute, they will be coming toward him as well. He yearns to know if it was his dad who helped him before. "Come on!" he mutters. "Where are you? Dad, come on—"[16] But his dad doesn't come. And suddenly it hits him— he realizes it wasn't his father he saw on the other side of the lake, it was himself. *He* had summoned the Patronus, and the Patronus was his father's spirit, a huge stag known to his intimate friends, Lupin, Black, and Pettigrew, as Prongs.

"Expecto patronum!" yells Harry. And this time, out of the end of his wand comes not a faint silvery mist as before but "a blinding, dazzling, silver animal." It looks like a horse, galloping around the lake, but it isn't. He sees it lower its head and charge at the dementors, and watches them fall back, scattering and retreating into the darkness until they are gone. The enormous stag stops by the water, stares at him with its huge silvery eyes, then lowers its head and vanishes.

Is it a ghost, as Hermione suggested? Or a memory, one so strong it is able to dispel the horrible dementors? Or a reincarnation of the great Prongs, summoned to help Harry in his hour of need? Elizabeth Schafer suggests that the Patronus "could be a magical descendant of the Roman patronus who protected selected individuals in Britannia."[17] Regardless, we can be sure that the derivation of the word from the Latin *pater* ("father") or Greek *patrowos* ("paternal, received from one's ancestors") is important. Harry's father, though dead since Harry was a year old, is somehow instrumental in protecting and saving him.

The silvery light that occurs with the Patronum is an interesting touch. One of the distinguishing marks of the life-after-life experience, according to Morton Kelsey in *Afterlife: The Other Side of Dying*, is the appearance of a bright light or of "a being of light" which is experienced somewhat as the disciples of Jesus appear to have experienced his transfiguration. Betty J. Eadie, in the immensely popular account of her afterlife adventure called *Embraced by the Light*, remembers the doctor's declaring her dead and pulling the covers over her head. Yet she was still seeing the doctor and the nurse standing by her bed.

> I looked around the room and noticed that it was filled with brighter light than before. The bed seemed huge to me, and I remember thinking, "I'm like a little brown bug in this big white bed." Then the doctor walked away and I became aware of another presence nearby. Suddenly I wasn't lying on the bed but found myself in someone's arms. I looked up and saw a man with a beautiful white beard looking at me. His beard fascinated me. It seemed to sparkle with a bright light, a light that came from within the beard.[18]

In the Tibetan Book of the Dead, it is said that the *bardo* body (literally, the body "between two") takes three or four days to detach itself from the physical body and proceed on its journey. During this time it is surrounded by an intensely bright light, blinding even, which is the "Radiance of the Clear Light of Pure Reality." If the person who has died is ready utterly and completely to abandon ego existence and become one with the Light, then it attains salvation and never returns to the life it has left. But only those who have come close to the total purification of the self in this life are really prepared to make this transition. The majority of souls passing through the bright Light are unwilling to be absorbed by it and remain in a state of Nirvana forever.

When Harry sees the bright light in connection with his father's presence, it is a symbol of the beyond, and the purity of the state from which he returns. By contrast, the atmosphere around the Death Eaters and the dementors is always dark and foreboding. It is a classical dualism, in which the good is always bright and shining, the evil, somber and menacing.

Again in *Harry Potter and the Goblet of Fire* we see Harry's parents coming to his aid, when he is in the life-and-death battle with Voldemort in the cemetery. Five ghosts appear out of the end of Voldemort's wand after his wand and Harry's have had a "reverse effect" on each other. First comes Cedric Diggory, Voldemort's most recent victim. Then Frank Bryce, the Muggle who stumbled unwittingly on Voldemort and Wormtail at the old Riddle mansion in Little Hangleton. Then Bertha Jorkins, a witch from the Ministry of Magic. And finally Harry's father and mother. His father first, "the smoky shadow of a tall man with untidy hair," and then his mother, "a young woman with long hair" and also in "smoky, shadowy form."

The voices with which they speak to Harry are "distant" and "echoing." They urge him to hold on, not to let go, to fight Voldemort to the end. His mother, walking close to him, speaking low so that Voldemort does not hear, tells him to get to the Triwizard Cup, the Portkey, and return to Hogwarts. And when his father gives him the signal, Harry breaks his wand's connection with Voldemort's and runs as fast as he can, zigzagging behind headstones, dodging curses and graves, until he reaches Cedric's body. He points his wand back over his shoulder and bellows, *"Impedimenta!,"* stopping at least one of the Death Eaters in pursuit. In the nick of time, he raises his wand toward the Triwizard Cup and shouts, *"Accio!"* The cup sails into the air and soars toward him. He grabs its handle and presto, he and Cedric's body are speeding back toward Hogwarts, out of the grasp of the Dark Lord!

The writer of the ancient book of Hebrews, faced with the need to stanch the flow of fearful believers abandoning the Christian faith, addressed a circular epistle to the early churches in which he cataloged the great line of the faithful all the way from Abel, Noah, and Abraham, through Moses, Rahab, David, and Samuel, to the courageous believers of his own day. Time would fail him to tell, he wrote, of all who had "conquered kingdoms, administered justice, obtained promises, shut the mouths of lions, quenched raging fire, escaped the edge of the sword, won strength out of weakness, become mighty in war, put foreign armies to flight."

Others were tortured, refusing to accept release.... Others suffered mocking and flogging, and even chains and imprisonment. They were stoned to death, they were sawn in two, they were killed by the sword, they went about in skins of sheep and goats, destitute, persecuted, tormented—of whom the world was not worthy. They wandered in deserts and mountains, and in caves and holes in the ground.[19]

These, says the writer, lived by faith even before they knew Christ, who was the fulfillment of all the promises made to them. "Therefore," he concludes his peroration, "since we are surrounded by so great a cloud of witnesses, let us also lay aside every weight and the sin that clings so closely, and let us run with perseverance the race that is set before us, looking to Jesus the pioneer and perfecter of our faith, who for the sake of the joy that was set before him endured the cross, disregarding its shame, and has taken his seat at the right hand of the throne of God."[20]

The ghostly personalities around Harry Potter are *his* cloud of witnesses, his encouragers in the struggle against Voldemort. They have suffered at Voldemort's hand but do not flinch in the continued battle against the evil one. They are Harry's helpers in a conflict as old as persecution itself. There can be no doubt that they will be there all the way, whether the end comes with the seventh novel in the series or lies beyond it. They belong to the forces of good, and good will always be pitched against evil, until the last syllable of recorded time.

IS THERE A RESURRECTION IN THE STORIES?

Harry Potter is a wounded hero, carrying Voldemort's scar on his forehead the way Christ bore the marks of the nails in his hands. But can he be said in any way to be resurrected, as Christ was resurrected? We noted earlier how, in *Harry Potter and the Sorcerer's Stone,* Harry lies in a trance or coma for three days following his violent struggle with Professor Quirrell and Voldemort. Is this in itself a symbol of resurrection? And if so, is it in any way connected with the continued vitality of the dead persons in the stories?

Our answer, in the absence of more definitive clues, must of course be tentative. Even if Rowling were consciously working with the core beliefs of the Christian faith, she would preserve the shadow and mystery of creativity, refusing to make the relationship over-plain. And the truth is that even in biblical faith the relationship between Christ's resurrection and the redemption of the dead is not as clear as Christians would often like it to be.

Professor John Hick of Cambridge University, in his scholarly *Death and Eternal Life,* cites the problems inherent in ascertaining exactly what the New Testament means by its use of the word *resurrection.* "There is a spectrum of possibilities," he says:

> Did the dead body of Jesus come forth from its grave to resume a fully physical life? Or was it somehow changed in

the tomb so that whilst retaining some physical attributes—
including shape, solidity, and the capacity to speak and
eat—it took on other contra-physical attributes such as the
capacity suddenly to materialize and dematerialize at points
in space? Should we draw upon the stories of supernatural
powers developed by great spiritual masters of the east
enabling them to exert an extraordinary control over their
own bodies and even to materialize and dematerialize at
will, and think of Jesus' resurrection as exhibiting an
extreme form of this kind of psychic power? Or did the resurrection consist in visions seen by some of Jesus' disciples
shortly after his death? If so, were the visions produced in
their minds by the living spirit of Jesus? Did the resurrection appearances thus belong to the category, familiar in the
annals of psychical research, of 'veridical hallucinations' in
which telepathically received information is presented to
consciousness in the form of visions? Or—moving further
along the range of possibilities—instead of there having
been either perception or visions, did the resurrection take
place entirely on the inner plane of the disciples' faith? Was
it a resurrection of their faith, or its elevation from a faith in
Jesus as their earthly leader to faith in Jesus as God's chosen
messenger, later becoming expressed in more readily com-
prehensible stories of visions and voices? And if so, is this
powerful resurgence of faith to be attributed to the activity
of the living spirit of the Lord; or to purely natural causes,
such as wishful thinking and self-deception? Or to his spirit
working through some such psychological mechanism?[21]

Before this bewildering array of possibilities, cited by Professor Hick not to discourage belief but to remind us of the problems we often face when attempting to reach absolute certainty about anything as metaphysical and significant as the resurrection, we can surely conclude that it is not necessary to specify exactly *how* resurrection and the afterlife are related in the Harry Potter stories in order to believe that they *are* somehow related—that Harry, as a Christ figure, brings the hope and assurance of the resurrection into the arena of human mortality and the whole question of an existence beyond the grave.

Voldemort, the Death Eaters, and the dementors represent the power and nature of death, in whose presence we constantly live. The dementors, especially, recall the shadowy world of the dead in Greek mythology, where ghosts are mere shades of their former selves, no longer empowered for living, and also the gloomy region of *Sheol* in Hebrew-Christian thought, which is likewise a place of sadness, darkness, unfulfilled longing, nagging regret, and utter powerlessness. When the boggarts appear to Harry, it is the dementors he sees; his fears take the form of their gray, scabby exteriors, with skin stretched over the holes where their eyes should be and mouths that suck hungrily at the very souls of others, wanting to devour everything that has feature and personality. This is because Harry is the hero of the opposite of death. He represents life and hope to all the good wizards and witches. Every time he survives a battle with Voldemort, it is an eschatological achievement, equal to a resurrection.

J. K. Rowling has said that her favorite painting is "perhaps" Caravaggio's *Supper at Emmaus,* which features Christ revealing himself to the disciples as the one who has just been raised from the dead. "I love it," she commented. "Jesus looks very likeable—soft and rounded—and the painting captures the exact moment when the disciples realize who this man is, blessing their bread."[22]

This is very revealing of an inner attitude we don't often get in interviews with Ms. Rowling. It seems to radiate a quiet reverence for the resurrection and all it stands for, which can explain a lot about her understanding of life and death and how they are related in the plots of her novels. If this is correct, it means that a great deal is riding on the faithfulness of Harry as a Christ figure, and what happens to him in future stories will essentially parallel what happened to Jesus.

AND NOW ABIDETH
FAITH, HOPE, AND LOVE

CHAP. 6.

N CHRIST CHURCH, Oxford, there is a beautiful window in the pre-Raphaelite style depicting *FIDES*, *SPES*, and *CARITAS*—faith, hope, and love. *Faith* is holding one of those little clay lamps common in biblical times. At her feet writhe dragon-snakes. One serpent is even entwining the hand not supporting the lamp. But she looks completely unafraid. *Hope* has a light, airy appearance. She is standing on tiptoe and gazing upward, as if she were dancing. *Love* is a mother with a small child in her arms and two others peering around her skirt. In her free hand she holds a flame burning high—a flame representing both the hearth and the future.

Rowling may well prefer Caravaggio's painting of Christ with the disciples at Emmaus. But this window, with its dragon-snakes, its mother protecting her children, and its indomitable sense of hope and expectancy, is a perfect tableau for the Harry Potter stories. The reptilian character of Voldemort and the Slytherins is there. So is Lily Potter's undying care for her son. And so is joyous hope—an undying confidence in the human enterprise—represented by the students at Hogwarts and especially by Harry Potter himself, who, despite all obstacles and punishments, tackles life the way he does a match of Quidditch, with an ever-growing sense of destiny and excitement!

Why have the Potter novels struck such a resonant chord in hearts around the world? The question must be asked. There are even Harry Potter Withdrawal Clubs, to console avid readers between the dates when the novels appear. Is Harry Potter only a trend like Pet Rocks, Hula-Hoops, and Frisbees? Or is there some deeper reason, something that strikes to the heart of who we are as human beings living on the cusp of two centuries, one recently concluded and the other barely opened?

The answer may lie in a book by Phil Cousineau called *Once and Future Myths: The Power of Ancient Stories in Modern Times.* Cousineau describes an exchange with psychiatrist Rollo May at May's home in Tiburon, California, shortly before his death in 1991. He asked May whether the current authorities on the way the world works—science, media, and technology—can ever satisfy the human need for meaning. With a sadness in his voice that Cousineau found startling, May said it was precisely a *nothingness,* a *lack* of meaning in contemporary life, that had driven most of his clients into therapy. He described what he heard from them as "a cry for myth," for great, overarching patterns that explain why things are the way they are. Cousineau asked if May believed what Joseph Campbell was alluding to when he said, "People are always talking about looking for the meaning of life, when what they're really looking for is a *deep experience* of life." "Yes, yes," responded May, "but not only deep. Numinous."[1]

The Potter stories are rich with the human past—the wounded hero, the hero's journey, the quest for the Grail, mythical beasts, spells and incantations, exciting contests, noble tournaments, people who turn into animals, community rituals, learning that leads to power, the determined struggle against evil and darkness. The books are vivid, dynamic mosaics of all our dreams, hopes, and fears of whatever it is that has made us so uniquely human, but told with a freshness and transparency that permit us to enter the stories without being conscious of the fragments themselves, and *live* the dreams, hopes, and fears all over again, so that, without actually thinking about it, without feeling our pulses, we enjoy "a *deep experience* of life."

But not only deep—*numinous!*

Rowling's books put us in touch once again with the magic and mystery of life, the dimension beyond the ordinary, the sense of wonder that makes even commonplace experiences shine with the brilliance of celestial bodies. Everyday games become eternal contests, and run-of-the-mill children, the kind found on any playground or in any classroom, are metamorphosed into adolescent heroes and heroines. Ordinary animals sprout wings, grow horns, become mixed with other animals, to become the beasts of fairy tales and legends. Owls descend from all directions, bearing letters and packages, like fluttering, angelic messengers from heaven. A school is transformed into a mysterious castle with secret passageways, code words, hidden chambers, and a population of personable ghosts and goblins. Simple knowledge, the kind gained from books and teachers, translates directly into practical usage. Children battle with the enemies we have all faced—unbearable cousins, taunting classmates, mean and overbearing teachers, *dull* teachers, loneliness, unattractiveness, failure, intractable evil—and *win!*

What isn't to like? What isn't to be mesmerized by?

"I'm not a child," one adult told me, "but I love Harry Potter. I think I can become as engrossed in the stories as a child can, because they put me in touch with all the feelings I had as a child. And not only that, but with all the feelings I have as an adult. When I lay down one of the Harry Potter stories, I look at life differently. It has more color, more brilliance, more pizzazz! I don't become Harry Potter. Maybe more Hermione. But I think I feel a lot more youthful, and have a spring in my step that wasn't there before. It's been a long time since I read or watched anything that did that for me. In fact, I'm not sure if anything ever did it before."

Probably what happens to Potter readers is what writer Diane Ackerman calls "deep play"—an involvement in life that is so complete, so absorbing, that it promotes great relaxation and enables the very cells of the mind and heart to renew themselves. It even involves "rapture and ecstasy," two qualities human beings need in order to feel whole and truly alive.

And it *always*, Ackerman says, "involves the sacred and holy, sometimes hidden in the most unlikely or humble places—amid towering shelves of rock in Nepal; crouched over print in a dimly lit room; slipping on Astro Turf; wearing a coconut-shell mask."[2]

This is what I have been insisting about the presence of Christian mythical structure in the Harry Potter literature. It isn't all that's there—not by any means. There are ancient Greek, Persian, Egyptian, and Roman mythologies, archaic British and European lore and legend, simple folktales and fairy stories from all over the world, all thrown together like the stuff in a child's locker, so that some of it is bent and some is jammed into other objects and most of it would be almost impossible to restore to its original shape. But also there, as a conscious or unconscious framework for everything, is the worldview without which none of it would really work for Rowling's readers because it is, after all, *the* worldview of the Western hemisphere, the basic structure of the Christian faith.

That faith is multifold and complex. Scholars and leaders have been working on it since its simple beginnings, if indeed they were simple, in first-century Palestine, coaxing and caressing the texts until the books, scrolls, tapes, and films about it, all gathered together, would probably fill the Bibliothèque Nationale in Paris, the Bodleian Library in Oxford, and the Library of Congress in Washington, D.C. Now the Christian faith is a lot like the Hebrew religion, which preceded it, as described by a legend about the simple shepherd's pipe once played by Moses when he kept his father-in-law's flocks.

When the pipe was discovered, many years after Moses' death, it was decided that it should be put on display for the benefit of his admirers. But it looked far too common for such an important purpose, so someone suggested that it be embellished by an artist. A few centuries later, when the pipe was given a new home in an upscale museum, a committee said it needed improving yet again. So another artist was employed to overlay it in fine gold and silver filigree. The result, in the end, was a breathtaking piece of art, a marvelous sight indeed. It was so beautiful, in fact, that no one ever noticed that it was no longer capable of the clear, seductive notes once played upon it by Moses.

That is the way of all religions. With the best of intentions, they become increasingly complicated until they lose the enchantment that was once their divine warrant. But of all the creeds in Christendom—Apostles', Nicene, Anti-Nicene, and all the rest—there is probably no truer or more dynamic one than the brief statement of faith St. Paul wrote to the Corinthians early in Christianity's history: "And now faith, hope, and love abide, these three; and the greatest of these is love."[3]

The window in Christ Church, Oxford, is a picture of this creed. And so are the Harry Potter novels!

FAITH

Faith is shown, in the window, heedless of the dragon-snakes around her. In other words, faith lives amid evil as if the evil were not there. It lives as seeing beyond evil, as though evil, powerful and destructive as it is, is only temporary. In the end, good will prevail; faith believes this, utterly and completely. Faith, in the classic definition from the book of Hebrews, is "the assurance of things hoped for, the conviction of things not seen."[4] It is a fundamental assumption that makes life both bearable and enjoyable.

We can sense this in the Potter stories as Harry, like St. George in the medieval stories, sticks it to the dragons. There is an implicit belief in the world order conceived by the good wizards, and this belief governs all their actions. They often brush with disaster, yet always with the confidence that their way is right. Any alternative is inconceivable. Another way would lead to death.

Lord Voldemort—"You-Know-Who"—and his followers serve only to assure the good people that they view the world in the correct way. The very name of Voldemort's disciples—Death Eaters—is symbolic of their position. They swallow death the way fire-eaters swallow fire. It is not a normative, faithful way to live. It is negative, the shadow side of all that is good and holy, and exists only as the counterpoint to the way of Dumbledore and his friends.

Albus Dumbledore, Gandalf-like, is the nearest thing to a true father figure in the novels. He is almost like God presiding over the affairs of the faithful. He is there when the infant Harry is brought to the Dursleys' house, turning out the street lamps and then turning them on again, as if he is in charge of the light. He is gentle, knowing, wise, unflappable, kind, and tolerant. Like a merciful heavenly Father, he overlooks Harry's boyish propensity for bending rules and getting into scrapes, and sees instead his inner nature and his importance in the overall scheme of things. He can become strong and wrathful (again like the heavenly Father), as he does with Cornelius Fudge, the Minister of Magic, near the end of *Harry Potter and the Goblet of Fire.* His eyes are said to blaze as he and Fudge disagree over what must be done to save the world from Voldemort and his minions. Knowing that Voldemort will try to enlist the giants for his dark purposes, he insists that Fudge make overtures to the giants and win their allegiance. Like a true bureaucrat, Fudge becomes visibly nervous about the consequences of such a step.

"If the magical community got wind that I had approached the giants," he gasps, shaking his head, "—people hate them, Dumbledore—end of my career—"

" 'You are blinded,' says Dumbledore forcefully, *his voice rising now, the aura of power around him palpable, his eyes blazing once more,* 'by the love of the office you hold, Cornelius! You place too much importance, and you always have done, on the so-called purity of blood! You fail to recognize that it matters not what someone is born, but what they grow to be!' "[5]

Rowling's treatment of bureaucracy is scathing. When the Quidditch World Cup matches are played in *Harry Potter and the Goblet of Fire,* the Ministry of Magic officials are in their element, arranging the venue, the seating, the camping, the amenities, the Portkeys to transport people, and everything else that must be seen to for a smoothly run show. Percy

Weasley, who aspires to ministry work, is ecstatic at the opportunities for serving the organization and becoming known to the various ministers. His father, Arthur Weasley, who already works at the ministry, gives Harry and Hermione, new to most of it, a rundown on the people they see passing them—Cuthbert Mockridge, Head of the Goblin Liaison Office, Gilbert Wimple, with the Committee on Experimental Charms, Arnold Peasegood, member of the Accidental Magic Reversal Squad, and Bode and Croaker, who are Unspeakables. When Harry and Hermione want to know what Unspeakables are, Weasley replies that they're from the Department of Mysteries, which is top secret, and that he has "no idea what they get up to."[6]

Fudge, as head of the Ministry of Magic and therefore chief bureaucrat, appears from time to time through the novels, almost always as the beneficent administrator, the superintendent who strolls through his provinces making sure that things are running efficiently and no one is unhappy with the Ministry's efforts. A shallow and generally benign man, he is concerned above all with avoiding gaffes and cock-ups, and with appearing to be managing everything well. When Sirius Black escapes from Azkaban, in *Harry Potter and the Prisoner of Azkaban,* and everybody thinks he is planning to kill Harry, Fudge seeks out Harry in Diagon Alley, where he and the Weasleys have gone to purchase their school supplies before the opening of the term. Harry is upset, because back at the Dursleys' he cast a spell on Aunt Marge that inflated her monstrously, and he thinks Fudge will tell him he is expelled from Hogwarts for unauthorized use of wizardry around Muggles. But Fudge behaves avuncularly, tut-tutting what has happened, feeding him buttered crumpets, and securing him a room at the Leaky Cauldron hostelry for the remainder of his vacation time. Harry doesn't realize until much later that Fudge is only trying to make sure he is okay so there won't be any chance of a screwup before Black is recaptured and returned to Azkaban. Like most experienced managers, Fudge is a slick politician who keeps his post by trying to quell trouble before it starts.

In *Harry Potter and the Goblet of Fire*, Fudge and the other bureaucrats are thrown into instant panic by the unexpected appearance of Voldemort's sign, "the Dark Mark," a large skull with a serpent for a tongue, in the night sky over the World Cup site. The area from which it emanated is instantly surrounded by a kind of wizard SWAT team, with police crashing through the underbrush in search of the perpetrator or perpetrators. The bureaucracy is on the side of goodness and decency and must always be seen to be upholding law and order. But, like all bureaucracies, it operates more out of concern for self-preservation than out of any deep commitment to moral order in the universe.

Dumbledore, on the other hand, is quietly, deeply, and passionately committed to the moral order, and presides over Hogwarts as the unshakable foe of darkness and evil. Harry seems to know this automatically, as a given in his nature.

When everybody, including himself, thinks Black is after him, he agrees wholeheartedly with Mrs. Weasley that "the safest place on earth" for him to be is wherever Dumbledore happens to be. "Didn't people always say that Dumbledore was the only person Lord Voldemort had ever been afraid of?"[7] And when Harry faces Tom Riddle in *Harry Potter and the Chamber of Secrets,* and Tom tells him he fashioned a new name for himself, Lord Voldemort, so that one day, when he had become the greatest wizard of all, other wizards would be afraid to speak it, Harry's mind turns instinctively to Dumbledore as his salvation:

> Harry's brain seemed to have jammed. He stared numbly at Riddle, at the orphaned boy who had grown up to murder Harry's own parents, and so many others. . . . At last he forced himself to speak.
>
> "You're not," he said, his quiet voice full of hatred.
>
> "Not what?" snapped Riddle.
>
> "Not the greatest sorcerer in the world," said Harry, breathing fast. "Sorry to disappoint you and all that, but the greatest wizard in the world is Albus Dumbledore. Everyone says so. Even when you were strong, you didn't dare try and take over at Hogwarts. Dumbledore saw through you when you were at school and he still frightens you now, wherever you're hiding these days—"[8]

And Harry's relation to Dumbledore is almost like that of a son to a father, for Dumbledore takes the deepest interest in

Harry and his development. There is a strong paternal feeling on his part for this remarkable child, and he seems to guide Harry with the right saying or the right gesture at precisely the right moment of his need.

I have not said this until now, for it could appear extremely far-fetched and ridiculous, and I have not felt like taking the risk. But suppose—just suppose—there is more significance to Harry's name than Rowling's casual remarks about it have led us to suspect. She once had some childhood friends named Potter, she says—Ian and Vikki Potter. And Harry—Harry's merely "a good, British name," isn't it? But consider—H.P. could stand for *huios pater*, Greek for "son" and "father" (the genitive of *pater* is *pateros*), something Rowling with her classics background would surely know. And Potter, as she would also know from her easy familiarity with European romance languages, is pronounced *pot-ter* in them, with an almost equal accent on both syllables, so that it sounds nearly identical to the Greek *pater*. Her hero could hardly be called Huios—it would be too obvious and would summon unwanted attention to itself. Huey, perhaps. But Harry is indeed a good old British name. One of two kings named Harold died at the Norman invasion of England in 1066. And isn't Harry the name of the youngest son of Prince Charles and Princess Diana? Born in 1984, he was about the same age as Harry Potter when the first Potter novel appeared.

As I said, it sounds far-fetched. Why make so much of Harry Potter's simple name? But the possibility is there— Harry, the Christ figure, and Albus Dumbledore, the Father figure. Rowling has said a number of times how excited she became when she first got the idea of the Potter stories while stalled on a train between London and Manchester for several hours. Could this symbolism have had anything to do with her excitement?

The strong sense of faith in the novels doesn't require such an identification to confirm it. It is there, whether the Son-Father thing is true or not. But I can't entirely dismiss the notion of its being true. Rowling is extremely clever, and it wouldn't be unlike her to disguise the religious meaning in her writings. She is also a very intuitive writer—which means that she could have introduced the meaning without thinking about it.

HOPE

Mainline Christianity has never made very much of the apocalyptic and eschatological elements in the New Testament because, as mainline and established, it doesn't have much interest in changing the status quo. It has focused instead on the structural and moral aspects of Jesus and the Apostles' teachings—on how Christians should behave, how they should regard non-Christians and the "world," and how they should pray and conduct their spiritual affairs. But objective scholarship is forced to admit that there is a very heady strain of apocalypticism in the Gospels, certain of the Epistles, and the book of Revelation, which is of course also known as the Apocalypse.

On the face of the evidence, Jesus apparently believed that the world would end soon after his death—perhaps even simultaneously with it—and that the kingdom of God would immediately appear. It is possible, of course, that most of the eschatological talk was put into Jesus' mouth by his followers after he died. But regardless of how they got there, there are large segments in the Gospels—notably Matthew 24–25 and Mark 13—that deal almost exclusively with the cataclysmic end of civilization.

That this bracing theme still holds a great deal of power for some is witnessed by the extraordinary popularity in recent years first of Hal Lindsey's book *The Late Great Planet Earth* and its spin-offs, and then of the Tim Lahaye–Jerry Jenkins *Left Behind* series, about the rapture of the faithful before God destroys the world and the universe. (At last count, the latter had sold approximately 30 million copies.) Both *The Late Great Planet Earth*, which is nonfiction, and the Lahaye–Jenkins books, which are novels, stem from a Pentecostalist emphasis on Revelation, with apocalyptic elements from the Old Testament book of Daniel thrown in. Largely ignored by mainline clergy and teachers, they have nevertheless won an enormous following among fringe churches and charismatic groups.

In the early church, Jesus was undeniably associated with the Eschaton, or end-time, when God would bring all history to a conclusion and the dramatic events symbolized in the book of Revelation would occur. His messiahship brought fresh hope and expectation to many who had begun to believe that the promises of the prophets would never be fulfilled.

This is the reason for the ecstatic speech of Simeon, the aged prophet who beheld the infant Savior in the temple. "Master," he said, "now you are dismissing your servant in peace, according to your word; for my eyes have seen your salvation."[9] The coming of Christ embodied the centuries-old hopes and aspirations of the Jewish people.

As John Sanford, the internationally known Jungian analyst, has written, the story of Christ's victory on the cross over the dominion of evil is "the most hopeful statement in the spiritual lore of humankind. It makes of Christianity an ultimately hopeful religious faith: no matter how great the darkness, no matter how powerful are the forces of senseless destruction, there is an essential divinity at the core of life that no power in heaven or earth can destroy."[10]

A similar sense of hope centers on Harry Potter in the Potter narratives. There is something electric in people's voices when they meet him. The story of his first encounter with Lord Voldemort, and the reflex action of Voldemort's Avada Kedavra curse, so that it nearly finished off Voldemort himself, has quickly become part of the wizard community's general knowledge. Good wizards everywhere, even in France and northern Europe, as we learn when the champions from those areas descend on Hogwarts for the Triwizard Tournament, recognize Harry's name and know of his special stature in the war with the Dark Lord. Just as Jesus was important to his followers in the first century as the symbolic opponent of evil and darkness in the world, Harry is important to the good people who know him in Rowling's fictional world.

There is a strong eschatological flavor to all of Rowling's novels. However funny or trivial the things that are going on in the foreground may be, they are set against the dark backdrop of conflict and potential disaster in the wizard realm. Voldemort is dangerous and threatening, even in a state of half-life, and there is always the worry that he will gather power again and disrupt everything. This is why there is so much panic and consternation when the Dark Mark appears in the sky over the Quidditch World Cup field near the beginning of *Harry Potter and the Goblet of Fire*. The sign has not been seen for years, and people had hoped it would never be seen again. Later in the novel, Professor Karkaroff interrupts Professor Snape's class because he is profoundly alarmed at the intensification of the Dark Mark on his arm, the one with which Voldemort branded his disciples. He and Snape both know it means that Voldemort is staging a return to power, and they dread it because it throws their lives into jeopardy. The Dark Lord never lets former disciples go. Part of them is bound to him forever.

Death and its minions are always ugly and menacing in the novels. Voldemort himself, when we meet him in *Harry Potter and the Sorcerer's Stone,* occupies the back of Professor Quirrell's head, like a ghoul, and forces Quirrell to drink the unicorn blood in order to make him stronger. The unicorn is a symbol of Christ and purity, so the act has something of the grotesque and witches' sabbath about it. When Frank Bryce stumbles upon Voldemort, Wormtail, and the snake "curled up on the rotting hearth rug, like some horrible travesty of a pet dog," in the first chapter of *Harry Potter and the Goblet of Fire*, he dares Voldemort to "turn 'round and face me like a man." Wormtail scoots the chair around so Bryce can see what is in it. The snake lifts its ugly head and hisses. And when Bryce sees the sight in the chair, his walking stick falls to the floor with a clatter and he screams so loudly that he doesn't even hear the words of the death curse spoken by "the thing in the chair" lifting its wand.

Voldemort's followers are also menacing and hateful. The Death Eaters, some of whom occupy important positions in the wizard government, are bitter and negative. The dementors, or soul-suckers, are utterly hideous. Harry's first encounter with one, on the train to Hogwarts in *Harry Potter and the Prisoner of Azkaban,* is shocking and unsettling. The lights on the train have gone out, and Professor Lupin, who is in the compartment with Harry, Ron, Hermione, and Neville, kindles some flames in his hand and starts for the door to see what is the matter. But the door slides open before he reaches it, and Harry sees a cloaked figure outside, so tall that it appears to reach the ceiling. Its face is completely hidden by the hood. Harry's eyes slide downward, and what they fall upon makes his stomach contract. There is a hand protruding from the cloak, and it is "glistening, grayish, slimy-looking, and scabbed," as if it were "something dead that had decayed in the water." The hand is withdrawn, and there is a long, slow, rattling sound, as if the creature were trying "to suck something more than air from its surroundings."[11]

Lupin later describes the Dementor's Kiss to Harry—how

the awful figure sucks the mind and soul out of its enemies, the way Tydeus, in the Greek myth, sucked the brain from the severed head of Melanippus (though Lupin doesn't mention Tydeus). He says he supposes there must be some kind of mouth under the hood, because the creature clamps its jaws on the mouth of the victim and sucks out the victim's soul.

"What—," says Harry, "they kill—?"

"Oh no," says Lupin. "Much worse than that. You can exist without your soul, you know, as long as your brain and heart are still working. But you'll have no sense of self anymore, no memory, no . . . anything. There's no chance at all of recovery. You'll just—exist. As an empty shell. And your soul is gone forever . . . lost."[12]

Voldemort, the Death Eaters, the dementors, the basilisk, the huge, ugly trolls, the dragons, snakes, spiders, grindylows, Blast-Ended Skrewts, and manticores, together with the Devil's Snare and other threatening plants, all paint an extraordinarily dark and threatening background for the Potter stories. They are one reason some parents won't let their children read Rowling's books. But they represent the shadow side of human existence, the horrible evil that contaminates and destroys people's souls, that binds and constricts them until, like the dementors' victims, they simply give up and live as the walking dead, no longer aware of a better way.

Harry, in the face of this, is fresh, strong, resourceful, and utterly resistant to evil. The lightning-shaped scar on his forehead, left by his original encounter with Voldemort, aches and throbs when something foul or malignant is about to occur—

sometimes so badly that it blinds him. It is an unfailing alarm to notify him of Voldemort's growing strength or threatening presence. It is Harry and his scar that Voldemort must destroy if he would possess the earth. Dumbledore, the wise and patient Father figure, realizes this, and casts all his power and knowledge behind Harry to defeat the Dark Lord. Harry is not only the knight-errant, he is the battleground. Like Christ on the cross, he suffers Voldemort's Cruciatus Curse, which makes him writhe on the ground in pain and distress. And twice, by the end of the fourth novel, he has been the target for Voldemort's Avada Kedavra curse. Everything is centered on him—the venom of Voldemort and the hope of the good wizards' survival. He is the eschatological figure of the novels, as Christ is of the Gospels, and all depends on him.

Not too long ago, Yale professor Henri J. M. Nouwen wrote a popular book called *The Wounded Healer*, whose thesis is that the best healers are those who have suffered wounds of their own but are prepared to take on the sufferings of others. This is essentially what Harry Potter is in the novels that bear his name: a wounded healer. Unlike Christ, whose wounding came at the end of his life, Harry's comes at the beginning, or very near the beginning. He already has the scar when we are introduced to him in the first story. Somehow, his power is tied up with the scar, just as Christ's was tied up with the nail holes in his hands; at least the scar bears evidence to his power. And he and his scar are the symbol of hope to the entire world of wizardry—the hope that, in the end, evil will be put down and good will triumph. Even at the end of the fourth novel, when things look so bleak for the good wizards, there is a sense of hope permeating everything. It is implicit even in Harry's gift of the Triwizard Cup prize money to Fred and George Weasley so they can buy a joke shop, and in his comment, "We could all do with a few laughs. I've got a feeling we're going to need them more than usual before long."[13]

I haven't commented much on the rich vein of humor running through the novels. But it is not unrelated to the business of eschatological hope. The thing that makes real humor possible—that is, true fun, joy, laugh-out-loud humor—is a strong confidence that everything is going to turn out okay. Humor doesn't work in dark or sad situations. For weeks after the tragic events of September 11, 2001, American humorists carefully toned down their monologues and certain funny movies were delayed for release because it was felt that the time wasn't right for the kind of frivolity and lightheartedness they purveyed. But humor is a wonderful tonic for tough times and bad days when we know that everything is going to come out all right in the end.

This is what Harry is talking about. Fred and George's practical jokes—Ton-Tongue Toffees, Canary Creams, fake wands—can make people laugh because there is light at the end of the tunnel. And much of that light is owing to Harry.

LOVE

Good and *evil* are nouns or adjectives. The verb forms of *good* are "to love" and "to help." The verb forms of *evil* are "to hate" and "to destroy." The cosmic struggle of good and evil therefore pit loving and helping against hating and destroying. Voldemort, Lucius Malfoy, and their associates are bent on hating and destroying the stability and structures of the wizard world. Dumbledore, Hagrid, Harry, and their friends are committed to saving them. The eschatological nature of the struggle arises from the fact that it is a struggle to the death. Evil takes no captives.

The ultimate goal of loving and helping is the essential unity of everything, while the goal of hating and destroying is the dismantling and dissolution of that unity. Lovers enjoy and celebrate. Haters scheme, besmirch, and try to overthrow. Lovers sacrifice themselves for the good of all. Haters destroy others for their own good. Lovers regard others as better than themselves. Haters have no consideration at all for others. Lovers tend to forgive offenses in others. Haters never forgive. They make a point of remembering.

Dumbledore is known for his forgiving nature. A wise and generous man, he has befriended the bumbling gamekeeper Hagrid for years, even though Hagrid was blamed for releasing the murderous creature from the Chamber of Secrets and dismissed from Hogwarts as a student. He brings Remus

Lupin back as a Professor of Defense Against the Dark Arts even though he knows Lupin is a werewolf and there would be outcries if others knew. He employed Severus Snape and trusts him as a colleague even though he knows that Snape was once branded by Voldemart's mark. He welcomes Professor Karkaroff from Durmstrang and displays every hospitality toward him although he knows that he too was once a servant of Voldemort. He repeatedly forgives Harry and his friends when they bend or break the rules of the school. He insists to Cornelius Fudge, the Minister of Magic, that they should send envoys to the giants, even though most wizards do not accept them.

Voldemort, on the other hand, is always full of bitterness and recriminations and forgives no one for anything. He hated Harry's parents from the time when they were students together and murdered them out of vengeance. He hates Harry because his Killing Curse on him failed and left Voldemort himself almost fatally wounded. He treats his servant Wormtail with loathing and contempt, frequently inflicting pain and humiliation on him, and requiring him in *Harry Potter and the Goblet of Fire* to cut off his hand in penance for not having been as faithful as he might. He berates Lucius Malfoy for not being a more visible, attentive servant. "I smell guilt," he hisses as he walks among the Death Eaters at the cemetery scene in *Harry Potter and the Goblet of Fire*. "There is a stench of guilt upon the air."[14] One of the Death Eaters flings himself at Voldemort's feet and shrieks, "Master, forgive me!

Forgive us all!"[15] Voldemort laughs, raises his wand, and pronounces the Cruciatus Curse on the follower, causing him to
writhe in torment on the ground.

Voldemort raises his wand and stops the curse. The poor
creature lies there, gasping.

"Get up, Avery," says Voldemort. "Stand up. You ask for
forgiveness? I do not forgive. I do not forget. Thirteen long
years . . . I want thirteen years' repayment before I forgive
you."[16]

Thirteen is the number of years since his curse on Harry
nearly destroyed himself, and is also an appropriate number
for a Dark Lord, as it is popularly associated with nefariousness
and evil. And perhaps it reminds us of another number, one
from the Gospels denoting extreme fullness:

> Then Peter came and said to him, "Lord, if another
> member of the church sins against me, how often should I
> forgive? As many as seven times?" Jesus said to him, "Not
> seven times, but, I tell you, seventy-seven times."[17]

In *Harry Potter and the Goblet of Fire,* Harry's power to
forgive is tested by his friend Ron's refusal to believe that
Harry didn't put his own name into the goblet as a candidate
for the Triwizard Tournament and the thousand-galleon prize.
Hermione tells Harry that Ron is only jealous, but Harry has
trouble forgiving a close friend who won't accept his word
without question. Like the two schoolboys they are, they continue to exchange rude remarks until the rift between them is

difficult to repair, and for several weeks they go their separate ways. Once, Harry hurls a "Potter Really Stinks" badge at Ron—one of Draco Malfoy's inventions—and hits him in the forehead. "There you go," says Harry. "Something for you to wear on Tuesday. You might even have a scar now, if you're lucky. . . . That's what you want, isn't it?"[18]

Their rapprochement occurs after Harry's hair-raising battle with the Horntail dragon in the first competition for the Triwizard Cup. It was a squeaker, and Harry could very well have lost his life. When Hermione and Ron come up to Harry afterward, Ron is white as a ghost. "Harry," he says, "whoever put your name in that goblet—I—I reckon they're trying to do you in!" "Caught on, have you?" Harry says, still smarting from Ron's earlier doubt. "Took you long enough." Hermione watches them both, fearful of what may happen. They stare at each other for a minute. Ron starts to open his mouth. Knowing what he's going to say, Harry stops him. "It's okay," he says. "Forget it." "No," says Ron, "I shouldn't've—" *"Forget it,"* says Harry.[19]

The whole episode is over, and the two boys begin to chatter together with the same affection they have always shared. Would it be pushing the envelope too much to say it is reminiscent of the reunion of Jesus and Simon Peter in Galilee after the crucifixion? Peter denied Jesus three times on the eve of his master's death. Three times, afterward, Jesus asked him, "Do you love me?" And three times Peter answered, "Lord, you know I love you."

Love also accounts, in the Potter narratives, for the way Harry, Hermione, and others accept people who are different from themselves. The Malfoys, father and son, are unyielding toward Muggles and Mudbloods—people who have any Muggle blood in them and aren't purebred wizards. But Harry and his friends are like Dumbledore, who says that it isn't how one is born that is important but what one makes of one's life. And Hermione, of course, mounts a campaign, in *Harry Potter and the Goblet of Fire*, to give the house-elves their freedom and compensation for their work, because she regards them as being of equal value with the wizards themselves. It is a sentiment that has its noble origins in a statement by St. Paul about the new regime in Christ: "There is no longer Jew or Greek, there is no longer slave or free, there is no longer male or female; for all of you are one in Christ Jesus."[20]

Real love, biblical love, is completely unselfish. The Greek word for love in the New Testament is always *agape* (generous love) or *philia* (love for a friend or sibling), never *eros* (sexual or acquisitive love). When asked what is the greatest commandment people are to live by, Jesus said:

> "The first is, 'Hear, O Israel: the Lord our God, the Lord is one; you shall love the Lord your God with all your heart, and with all your soul, and with all your mind, and with all your strength.' The second is this, 'You shall love your neighbor as yourself.' There is no other commandment greater than these."[21]

The use of the word *agape* here indicates a complete selflessness—basking in adoration with a delight beyond desire, and then loving the neighbor, or the other, in the same way. It is the height of spirituality, a merging of the soul in what Emerson called the Oversoul, a total surrender to the beauty and splendor of God and the creation. It is a love that overcomes all barriers, accepts and dissolves all opposites, embraces all contrarieties. It is what Frederick Buechner expresses in *The Alphabet of Grace* when he says:

> The language of God seems mostly metaphor. His love is like a red, red rose. His love is like the old waiter with shingles, the guitar-playing Buddhist tramp, the raped child and the one who raped her. There is no image too far-fetched, no combination of sounds too harsh, no spelling too irregular, no allusion too obscure or outrageous. The alphabet of grace is full of gutturals.[22]

In the mystical oneness of everything, that is, even the dissonances are absorbed and heard as something else. There is a shining, otherworldly quality to everything. The lover is embraced by it all, disappears in the folds of its embrace, dies of ecstasy in the arms of the other, which of course is no longer the other, because now they are one, and there is only the sound of one hand clapping left ringing in the air.

Lord Voldemort could not endure such talk. He would ridicule it as the sheerest idiocy.

But Harry would understand—and Dumbledore—and Hermione—and even Hagrid, who cares for baby dragons and Blast-Ended Skrewts and other aberrations of nature. They belong to the fellowship of loving, kindred spirits. They are open to the world as magic and mystery, as a field of delight for all who live in it. But because they are realists—because they see things with open eyes and are not blinded by romanticism—they are ready to sacrifice themselves to oppose the Dark Lords and dementors and Malfoys who would rob them and others of their simple pleasure in life. They know how imperiled the world is and will do whatever is required to stop Voldemort—even if it kills them.

But we are confident that it won't. Not all of them, at any rate. And the reason we're confident is that we already know the overarching plot of the novels. It is the plot of orthodox Christianity, now written into the unconscious of every Westerner, and perhaps even Easterners as well. Christ may die, but Christ will live, because in the end evil is less powerful than good, and Satan will lose out to God. It is that simple. It is the text to which all life resonates. "God was, in Christ, reconciling the world to himself."[23] God was making all things one—bundling all the magic and mystery into a unity, a single existence.

Harry—and all his readers, for that matter—must make the hero's journey and battle the evil forces in order to come to the full realization of this. As John Sanford says,

Good and evil will be curiously intermingled in any meaningful life process. If we are to become whole, life will send us, not what we want, but what we need in order to grow. The forces of evil will have to touch our lives, for without the dark Luciferian power, consciousness does not emerge, as Mephistopheles seems to be saying in Goethe's play *Faust* when he declares of himself that he is "part of that Force which would do evil ever, yet forever works the good."

Individuation is a work, a life opus, a task that calls upon us not to avoid life's difficulties and dangers, but to perceive the meaning in the pattern of events that form our lives. Life's supreme achievement may be to see the thread that connects together the events, dreams, and relationships that have made up the fabric of our existence. Individuation is a search for and discovery of meaning, not a meaning we consciously devise, but the meaning embedded in life itself. It will confront us with many demands, for the unconscious, as Jung once wrote, "always tries to produce an impossible situation in order to force the individual to bring out his very best."[24]

Once we have made the pilgrimage and slain the dragons along the way, as Harry does, we arrive at the kind of genteel wisdom possessed by Dumbledore, which is characterized by an extreme wariness of evil and, at the same time, a profound love for life and people. We accept life on its own terms—the evil with the good—and, like God in the creation narrative in Genesis, pronounce it "very good." We understand the mystical oneness of everything, and cherish it with a deep passion. We wish we could even embrace the Voldemorts and Malfoys and love them into unity with everything else, though we are realistic enough to know that they persistently choose damnation and would never agree to reunification. This is the one point at which the Christian vision sticks and can go no further, but must finally remain dualistic; it recognizes that evil cannot be entirely absorbed by good. The devil and his angels must be cast into the lake of everlasting fire, for they will never repent and become part of the beloved community.

But this does not allay the power of faith, hope, and love in our lives. Especially love. We see the world as miracle—Rowling has only just touched on its real magic—and adore it. We understand fellowship, and crave it. We feel the presence of God, and bow down. All life is sacrament, and, through the journey to individuation, our hearts are purged to receive it. With Harry Potter in his finest moments, we feel a sense of deep and quiet reverence, an obligation to all that is, and we know—we *know*—that evil cannot finally win. God—and Dumbledore?—are too great for that!

ABOUT THE AUTHOR

John Killinger, who holds doctorates in both theology and literature, has taught courses in the theological aspects of contemporary literature at Vanderbilt University, the University of Chicago, City College of New York, and Samford University. An ordained clergyman, he has been minister of the First Presbyterian Church in Lynchburg, Virginia, and the First Congregational Church of Los Angeles, California. He is presently a freelance writer and for the past seven years has served as minister of the Little Stone Church, a resort parish on Mackinac Island, Michigan. Among his many publications are several books in the field of literary criticism, including *Hemingway and the Dead Gods* (Lexington, Kentucky: University Press of Kentucky, 1960; Citadel, 1965); *The Failure of Theology in Modern Literature* (Nashville: Abingdon Press, 1963); *The Fragile Presence* (Philadelphia: Fortress Press, 1973); and *World in Collapse: The Vision of Absurd Drama* (New York: Dell, 1970). He has also written two novels, *Jessie* (New York: McCracken Press, 1993) and *The Night Jessie Sang at the Opry* (Centreville, Virginia: Angel Books, 1996), which feature Christ as a woman in modern times.

NOTES

Note: All quotes from the Harry Potter books are from the standard (hardcover) American edition, Arthur A. Levine Books, Scholastic Publications. All quotes from the Bible are from the New Revised Standard Version.

INTRODUCTION

1. Richard Abanes, *Harry Potter and the Bible* (Camp Hill, Pennsylvania: Horizon Books, 2001), 97.

2. Ibid., 241.

3. Ibid., 271.

4. Connie Neal, *What's a Christian to Do with Harry Potter?* (Colorado Springs, Colorado: Waterbrook Press, 2001), 50.

5. Ibid., 88.

6. Margo Jefferson, "Harry Potter for Grown-Ups," *The New York Times* (January 20, 2002).

7. Elizabeth Schafer, *Exploring Harry Potter* (Osprey, Florida: Beacham Publishing Co., 2000), 163.

8. Ibid., 164.

1. MYSTERIOUS BIRTHS AND MIRACULOUS CHILDHOODS

1. J. K. Rowling, *Harry Potter and the Sorcerer's Stone* (New York: Scholastic, 1998), 2.

2. Ibid.

3. Luke 2:48.

4. Matthew 12:46–50; Mark 3:31–35; Luke 8:19–21.

5. John 19:26–27.

6. *Sorcerer's Stone*, 13.

7. Ibid., 17.

8. Ibid., 12.

9. Luke 2:25–38.

10. *Sorcerer's Stone*, 16.

11. A. N. Wilson, *Jesus: A Life* (New York: W. W. Norton, 1992), 73.

12. Ibid., 84.

13. *Sorcerer's Stone*, 53.

14. Luke 4:1–11.

2. THE STRUGGLE BETWEEN GOOD AND EVIL

1. Matthew 13:24–30.

2. *Sorcerer's Stone*, 298.

3. Revelation 12:7–9, 13–17.

4. Acts 2:2–3.

5. Romans 8:19, 21.

6. J. K. Rowling, *Harry Potter and the Prisoner of Azkaban* (New York: Scholastic, 1999), 427.

7. J. K. Rowling, *Harry Potter and the Goblet of Fire* (New York: Scholastic, 2000), 733.

3. THE GAME OF LIFE

1. *Sorcerer's Stone,* 144.

2. Ibid., 167.

3. Abanes, *Harry Potter and the Bible,* 205–206.

4. Micah 6:8.

5. *Sorcerer's Stone,* 100.

6. J. K. Rowling, *Harry Potter and the Chamber of Secrets* (New York: Scholastic, 1999), 15.

7. Ibid.

8. Ibid., 110.

9. Matthew 19:17.

10. John 6:15.

11. Marcus Borg, *Meeting Jesus Again for the First Time: The Historical Jesus and the Heart of Contemporary Faith* (San Francisco: HarperSanFrancisco, 1994).

12. *Chamber of Secrets,* 328.

13. Luke 9:51.

14. *Chamber of Secrets,* 166–172.

15. *Sorcerer's Stone,* 291.

16. Ibid., 185.

17. Ibid., 188.

18. *Goblet of Fire,* 341.

19. Ibid., 139.

20. Ibid., 223.

21. Ibid., 224.

22. Ibid., 238.

23. Matthew 7:12.

24. John 15:12–13.

25. Matthew 20:28.

26. Jaroslav Pelikan, *Jesus Through the Centuries—His Place in the History of Culture* (New Haven, Connecticut: Yale University Press, 1985), 95.

27. *Sorcerer's Stone*, 177.

28. Ibid., 270.

29. Ibid., 283.

30. *Chamber of Secrets*, 179.

31. Ibid., 194.

32. Ibid., 301.

33. *Goblet of Fire*, 500.

34. John 15:13.

35. John 3:16.

36. 1 John 4:7–12.

37. *Sorcerer's Stone*, 299.

38. *Goblet of Fire*, 666–668.

39. Ibid., 722–723.

40. Ibid., 723.

41. Galatians 5:19–23.

42. *Chamber of Secrets*, 333.

43. Deuteronomy 30:19–20.

44. John 21:15.

45. *Goblet of Fire*, 708.

46. Lindsey Fraser, *Conversations with J. K. Rowling* (New York: Scholastic, 2000), 34–35.

47. Speaking of her marriage and divorce, Rowling said: "I've

made my mistakes in that area. Just because you've got a good brain doesn't mean you're any better than the next person at keeping your hormones under control." In Marc Shapiro, *J. K. Rowling: The Wizard Behind Harry Potter* (New York: St. Martin's Press, 2001), 60–61.

48. Fraser, *Conversations with J. K. Rowling*, 28.

49. Speaking to an interviewer, J. K. Rowling confirmed that Dementors represent the mental illness known as depression: "That is exactly what they are. It was entirely conscious. And entirely from my own experience. Depression is the most unpleasant thing I have ever experienced." In David Colbert, *The Magical Worlds of Harry Potter* (Wrightsville Beach, N.C.: Lumina, 2001), 57.

50. Romans 7:19.

51. Philippians 3:12.

4. THE MAGICAL, MYSTICAL WORLD

1. *Prisoner of Azkaban*, 100.

2. *Goblet of Fire*, 660–61.

3. Schafer, *Exploring Harry Potter*, 185.

4. Lawrence LeShan, *The Medium, the Mystic, and the Physicist* (New York: Ballantine Books, 1975), 5.

5. W. R. Inge, *Christian Mysticism* (Greenwich, England: Meridian Books, 1950), 24.

6. Stephen Hawking, *A Brief History of Time: From the Big Bang to Black Holes* (New York: Bantam, 1990), 10.

7. Ibid., 175.

8. Schafer, *Exploring Harry Potter*, 193.

9. Matthew Fox, *One River, Many Wells* (New York: Jeremy P. Tarcher/Putnam, 2000), 16.

10. Anne Lamott, *Traveling Mercies: Some Thoughts on Faith* (New York: Pantheon Books, 1999), 100.

11. Dag Hammarskjöld, *Markings* (London: Faber and Faber, 1964), 64.

12. Michael Mayne, *This Sunrise of Wonder: Letters for the Journey* (London: HarperCollins/Fount, 1995), 15.

13. Ibid., 22–23.

5. OF GHOSTS AND GOBLINS AND THE LIFE AFTER DEATH

1. Macrina Wiederkehr, *A Tree Full of Angels* (New York: HarperCollins, 1990), xii–xiii.

2. *Sorcerer's Stone,* 115.

3. *Chamber of Secrets,* 307–08.

4. Mayne, *Sunrise of Wonder,* 106.

5. Elizabeth Goudge, *Pilgrim's Inn* (New York: Coward-McCann, 1948), 314.

6. Leslie D. Weatherhead, *The Christian Agnostic* (Nashville: Abingdon Press, 1965), 266–67.

7. 1 Samuel 28:3–25.

8. John 20:19–23; 21:4–8.

9. Luke 24:13–27.

10. 1 Corinthians 15:6.

11. *Prisoner of Azkaban,* 427–28.

12. *Goblet of Fire,* 462.

13. Ibid., 496–97.

14. *Sorcerer's Stone,* 208–09.

15. *Prisoner of Azkaban,* 407.

16. Ibid., 411.

17. Schafer, *Exploring Harry Potter,* 177.

18. Betty J. Eadie, *Embraced by the Light* (Placerville, California: Gold Leaf Press, 1992), 5.

19. Hebrews 11:32–38.

20. Ibid., 12:1–2.

21. John Hick, *Death and Eternal Life* (London: William Collins Sons, 1976), 172–73.

22. Fraser, *Conversations with J. K. Rowling,* 30–31.

6. And Now Abideth Faith, Hope, and Love

1. Phil Cousineau, *Once and Future Myths: The Power of Ancient Stories in Modern Times* (Berkeley, California: Conari Press, 2001), 13.

2. Diane Ackerman, *Deep Play* (New York: Vintage Books, 1999), 13.

3. 1 Corinthians 13:13.

4. Hebrews 11:1.

5. *Goblet of Fire,* 708 [italics in the original].

6. Ibid., 86.

7. *Prisoner of Azkaban,* 67–68.

8. *Chamber of Secrets,* 314.

9. Luke 2:29–30.

10. John Sanford, *Mystical Christianity* (New York: Crossroad, 1994), 330.

11. *Prisoner of Azkaban,* 83.

12. Ibid., 247.

13. *Goblet of Fire,* 733.

14. *Goblet of Fire,* 647.

15. Ibid., 648.

16. Ibid., 649.

17. Matthew 18:21.

18. *Goblet of Fire,* 335–36.

19. Ibid., 358.

20. Galatians 3:28.

21. Mark 12:29–31.

22. Frederick Buechner, *The Alphabet of Grace* (New York: Seabury Press, 1970), 13.

23. 2 Corinthians 5:19.

24. John Sanford, *Healing and Wholeness* (Ramsey, New Jersey: Paulist Press, 1977), 20.